The Emerging Leader

Advance Praise for *The Emerging Leader*

"Emerging leaders are, literally, the future of business. **Fostering their growth is essential to any long-term strategy an organization might have.** But talent management is just now becoming a focus. Here, **Jamie powerfully bridges the gap between old world tenets and new world reality** to identify and develop those emerging leaders with the greatest potential."

—**Stephen M.R. Covey,** Author of the *New York Times* and #1 *Wall Street Journal* bestseller *The Speed of Trust*

"What do you know about your next generation of leaders—the up-and-coming leaders you rely on to keep your company thriving and competitive? Read Jamie Broughton's powerful new book *The Emerging Leader*, and **learn to spot, leverage, and lead your next generation of leaders to greater success.** In it, he tells you what you need to know and more!"

—**Marshall Goldsmith** is the *New York Times* bestselling author of *Succession: Are You Ready?* and *What Got You Here Won't Get You There*—a *Wall Street Journal* #1 business book

"The team with the best talent wins. Jamie's ideas can be **a secret competitive weapon to attract, develop, and retain the best people in your industry.** . . . He has proven techniques that develop emerging leaders to their fullest potential."

—**Cathy Honor,** Head of Canadian Insurance Businesses RBC Royal Bank

"**Great strategic leaders deal effectively with paradox and are willing to invest in the future.** By investing time and training, as well as providing developmental opportunities, we make emerging leaders more attractive to others and, in so doing, make our organization more attractive to them. **Developing such leaders is both strategic and paradoxical, and boy, being able to manage that paradox is powerful!** *The Emerging Leader* provides the guidance to do just that—absolutely recommended!"

—**W. Glenn Rowe,** PhD, Director, Executive MBA Program, Paul MacPherson Chair in Strategic Leadership, Richard Ivey School of Business

"This book **will help HR professionals clearly communicate the value and urgency of talent development inside their organizations.** Jamie's understanding of the Emerging Leaders' world nails it! He's done a great job highlighting the talent situation, its risks, and the benefits and value Emerging Leaders can provide. He then gives specific guidance on how senior executives can get out of the way and **unleash the potential that this important employee segment can offer.** If you're looking for a **practical response to deepening the pipeline of talent and getting the most out of people today** and for the future, this is the book for you!"

—**Jodi Drake,** VP Talent Management & Organizational Effectiveness, Aviva Canada Inc.

"Jamie Broughton offers to be your Sherpa to help you cross the crevasse of understanding that separates the Senior Leader and Emerging Leader worlds. You should take him up on his offer. **The world of coaching and leadership development has been over-complicated by many,** but like an experienced guide he simplifies the effort and takes the journey with you. His advice is clear and practical. He builds your confidence as he prods you to recognize the realities of the workplace and shows you how to successfully meet them. Packed with stories, examples, and clear advice, **the book takes you along one step at a time until you realize, this isn't rocket science after all!**"

—**Stanton Smith,** National Director, Cross Generational Initiatives, Major U.S. Global Consulting Firm. Author of: *Decoding Generational Differences: Fact, fiction . . . or should we just get back to work*

"If you haven't read *The Emerging Leader*, your up-and-coming employees are like sitting ducks, waiting to be picked off by an organization who understands them. Too many companies are realizing they don't know what they've got until it's gone. ***The Emerging Leader* helps** today's executives embrace the brave new world of tomorrow's workforce and **stop the talent leak that's costing companies millions of dollars a year.**"

—**Randy McGlynn,** CEO, Ontario Teachers Insurance Plan

"This book **presents a really compelling 'burning platform' for change** in terms of how organizations approach the critical issue of succession planning. Jamie's built a solid case outlining the demographics and the impact it will have on the workforce. The book will help busy executives understand that **if they just focus on the traditional high-priority 'business' issues** at the expense of succession planning, **they're going to be okay today and gone tomorrow.**"

–**Linda Duxbury,** PhD, Professor, Sprott School of Business, Carleton University, Change Management and Workplace Health Expert

"**Today more than ever, senior executives need to understand the impact they can have on their Emerging Leaders.** A key way to achieve this is to open their minds to a new coaching approach and accept the fact that these next generations are different and they are indeed our leaders of the future.

"**I wish I could offer this book to every senior leader** who's not fully conscious of their critical role to develop our future leaders, or doesn't know where to start. What Jamie's written is easy to read and apply."

–**Esther Auger,** Global Practice Director, Talent Management, The Hatch Group, Financial Post Canada's 50 Best Managed Companies Award 2007, 2008

"**We experience the best from people when they're engaged in their work.** Research has shown that the top two factors that impact engagement and satisfaction is the employee's relationship with their front-line manager and the opportunities they receive to develop their skills. *The Emerging Leader* tackles these factors head-on and helps established leaders **master the art of the long view by balancing the developmental needs of their emerging leaders with the shorter-term needs of the organization to get the work done.** Well worth the read!"

–**Wendy Macdonald,** Director Organizational Development, Sunnybrook Health Sciences Centre

"What determines whether a business is a success or simply 'a great idea that never made it' is its people. **Indentifying and developing promising talent needs to be a fundamental priority for every senior executive.** *The Emerging Leader* is the ***Men are from Mars, Women are from Venus*** **book for anyone charged with growing the next** (**and different**) **wave of leaders**—highly effective and practical!"

–**Mark A. Stein,** Senior Vice President, Gordon Brothers Group

"I relate to **Jamie's approach of engaging Emerging Leaders like the 'Tai-Chi of management'—go with where they are and use it to an advantage.** When organizations give up resisting the way the workplace is shifting and instead embrace the development and life needs of their future leaders within that workplace, they'll want to stay longer! It will be a win-win for everyone.

"Jamie clearly has a commitment and a passion for this work and it's very authentic. It's as much his story as it is the story of the Emerging Leaders. He has written this from a personal passion, a personal journey, and a personal desire to really create a legacy for the future. **If you've got questions about how to connect with and ignite your emerging leaders, read this book!** It's a practical guide to leveraging the strength of the emerging talent in your organization."

–**Jennifer Pierce,** VP Talent Management,
Hudson's Bay Company

"**I felt a chill of recognition** when I read this book! It functions like a window and a mirror for both the emerging leader and the senior leader. Not only can each examine themselves, they can see each other—causing a real breakthrough in understanding and trust. **The best thing that could happen is this book becomes required reading for both emerging and senior leaders,** especially before performance reviews and development discussions."

–**Sarah Kapoor,** Senior Producer, Canada's Next Great Prime Minister, 2007 & 2008 Programs, CBC Television

"This book is right on target! **It raises a very timely conversation, not only about our emerging leaders but indeed the emerging workplace.** It's easy to confuse understanding with wisdom and the fact that Jamie has lived this journey comes through loud and clear in the book. For any organization serious about developing their next generation of leaders, this is a must-read you'll refer to frequently!"

–**Rita Bailey,** CEO, QVF Partners and Founding Partner of Up To Something Partners, LLC, Former Director, Southwest Airlines University, Past Chair ASTD, Co-Author of *Destination Profit—Creating People Profit Opportunities in your Organization*

"An excellent book! Jamie's approach on developing people from inside spoke to me very much. **Many times organizations don't realize the value (and savings) of growing existing staff with potential.** If you're involved in planning for, or fulfilling on, your succession plan, *The Emerging Leader* is a great resource."

—**Walter Hachborn,** Founder,
Home Hardware Stores Limited

"If you think you have a lot of potential young leaders in your organization, but have not been able to capture that talent, *The Emerging Leader* can help! It **gives any manager the practical tools to work effectively with their promising talent** and move them forward as leaders in their company. Highly recommended."

—**Bob Hottman,** Chief Executive Officer,
EKS&H Certified Public Accountants and Advisors

"I'm constantly challenging my students with questions such as 'Is this practical? Can we use this? Will it help us? Is it going to enlighten us?' Jamie's book does all those things! **I could envision teaching a whole leadership program around this book.** For leaders planning the future of their organization and considering their influential role within it as educators, facilitators, or leaders, this is a must-read!"

—**Teal McAteer,** PhD, Professor, MBA Program,
DeGroote School of Business, McMaster University

"I think it is very important to continue to promote any materials supporting the need to put people first. This book continually promotes that message and focuses on **the senior leader job as the one that unleashes their ELs' potential.** You have provided insight into the mindset and the life of the EL workforce today and **drive what I consider to be a critical point—that life is now fluid, and enabling people to lean in and lean out as they need to** generally results in a team that integrates their work as part of their life. As this happens it is no longer work but another element of who they are and what provides meaning for them.

"In addition, I appreciate all books that promote curiosity and self-awareness. This book asks SLs to approach every discussion with an open mind, ready to hear what the ELs are recommending and listening with empathy versus judgment. I like how you have focused on this as the way to motivate and empower your organization."

—**Susanne Currie,** Country Manager, Procter & Gamble,
Oral Health

"**Anyone managing leaders under forty will want to rip out pages of this book for their briefcase!** Broughton provides the key for invigorating a dynamic workforce, especially for today's senior leaders fighting the talent war. His coaching starter kit is worth the price of the book alone. **I've already given a book to my boss!**"

—**George Langlois,** 2008 Top Forty Under 40 award recipient, *Ottawa Business Journal*

"Identification of talent is always part art and part science. ***The Emerging Leader* adds more science to the process** and reduces the "random factor."It also helps managers understand the important balancing point between employee and organization needs. **I've got a bunch of dog-eared pages in my copy** I'll refer back to again and again. **If talent development is a priority to you or your organization, this is a must-read!**"

—**Bruce Burrows,** Senior Vice President, Strategic Program Office, Loblaw Companies Limited

"As an Emerging Leader myself, I know full well that the stress of everyday life can be even bigger than the stress I have to deal with at work. It sometimes feels like I've already done an entire day's work before I arrive at nine in the morning. Your 'Day in the Life of an Emerging Leader' section completely resonated. **I recall thinking, 'Oh my gosh, that's me!'**

"**Jamie has literally created a road map on how to think about and approach emerging leaders.** Lightbulbs will go off for senior executives when they read this and understand that speaking their language is fundamental to getting (and keeping) them engaged. Otherwise, they're going to keep moving on. This will be **an eye-opener and absolutely recommended for anybody who is engaged in succession planning for leaders.**"

—**Heather Sauve,** AVP Customer Experience & Relationship Management, Canadian Operations, Sun Life Financial

"**There's been a lot of fanfare about the power of coaching, but I haven't seen much practical how-to guidance for people in leadership roles—until now.** For those leaders who want to begin coaching, sharpen their skills, or simply rekindle their interest in developing others, this is really the book for you!"

—**Stephanie Willson,** Chief Professional Resources Officer, McCarthy Tétrault LLP

"Jamie's book provides a concise understanding of what drives Emerging Leaders and gives senior leaders highly useful tools and models to maximize their output and loyalty. It **promotes mutual trust and respect** with both groups, which not only **gives the Emerging Leader a fair shake but also taps the tremendous experience the established leader brings to the table.** An excellent read!"

—**Darren Mahaffy,** Vice President Marketing,
Weston Bakeries Canada

"The war for talent means a lot of things, but it's mostly about creating an environment where people want to come and work. **Jamie shakes up traditional thinking and provides you with the essential elements to engage and retain your most important resource**—one that rides down the elevator on their way home every night—**your future leaders!**"

—**Nick Thadaney,** Chief Executive Officer,
ITG Canada Corporation

"**Jamie clearly understands the territory of the Emerging Leader** and the issues surrounding them—he's lived it personally and been inside their heads for years. **The challenges of retention, engagement and supply of quality talent are not going away.** Traditional leadership frameworks no longer serve.

"The early-adopters will harness the tremendous opportunity to embrace and engage their next generation of leaders as a competitive advantage that creates value for the organization and communities they serve. *The Emerging Leader* is a crucial resource to help you do just that!"

—**Victoria Wilding,** CEO, The SHIFT Foundation

"**It's simple—to grow as organizations we have to have great talent** and, frankly, talent that's better than the competition! **We also need to understand what makes that talent tick to get the best from them.** I'm 57 years old and have started planning for the next generation to take over. The problem is when I talk to my emerging leaders it's like we're on different planets; it's frustrating! Jamie's book provides a **valuable and eye-opening perspective on tackling the issue of growing our future leaders.**"

—**Les Mandelbaum,** President, Umbra

"This is extraordinary work! Jamie **provides a step-by-step 'how-to' manual for capturing the value of Emerging Leaders.** It also breathes of authenticity through the sharing of his own real world examples. He's done a superb job of taking experienced leaders from a 100,000-foot view down to practical application at ground zero.

"Although this is a guide for growing Emerging Leaders, it would be equally beneficial to anyone interested in developing their leadership skills. I highly recommend adding it to your bookshelf!"

—**Maureen Jillain,** Former Director, Leadership Development, ING Canada Inc.

THE EMERGING LEADER

Identify, Ignite and Retain Your Company's Next Generation of Leaders

JAMIE BROUGHTON

Footprint Publishing | Toronto

Footprint
PUBLISHING

Published by Footprint Publishing, www.footprintpublishing.com
Jacket design: Dunn+Associates, www.dunn-design.com
Cover photo: Justin Wu, www.jwuphoto.com
Interior design: Dorie McClelland, www.springbookdesign.com
Charts: Dunn+Associates, www.dunn-design.com

ISBN: 978-0-9812593-0-7

Printed in Canada by Friesen Corporation
14 13 12 11 10 01 02 03 04 05

Library and Archives Canada Cataloguing in Publication

Broughton, Jamie, 1969-
The emerging leader : identify, ignite and retain your company's next generation of leaders / Jamie Broughton.

ISBN 978-0-9812593-0-7

1. Leadership. 2. Success in business. I. Title.

HD57.7.B7635 2009 658.4'092 C2009-905418-3

For April
who inspired it all

For Simon and Samantha
and the future leaders they represent

For anyone
who's committed to make a difference in the world

THE EMERGING LEADER

Identify, Ignite and Retain Your Company's Next Generation of Leaders

Section III

Develop and Leverage Your Emerging Leaders

Introduction: The Elements of Performance:

The Human Capital Formula

Section IV

Coaching ELs to Success

Acknowledgments

This book would not have been started, let alone completed, without the tremendous support of dozens and dozens of people. To all of you I owe my deepest gratitude. What follows is certainly an incomplete list.

They say behind every successful person is a fantastic person supporting them. That couldn't be truer in my case. I begin my thanks with my incredible wife, April. Without you the journey would never have begun, and surely, without you we wouldn't have arrived. Your belief in me and your endless support in doing whatever was needed to make this project succeed are immeasurable. You are a continual source of inspiration, love and grace.

To my wide-eyed children, Simon and Samantha, who even at the ages of six and four get it that Dad's up to something he believes in. Thank you for all you're teaching me and the countless silent deliveries of juice, snacks and smiles to my office while creating this project—and indeed, being the ultimate reason I do this work.

Who are we without Mom and Dad? Without your bedrock of love and support over the years, this project, indeed this business, might never have happened. I can only hope to pay-forward your gift to the next generation as graciously as you bestowed yours on me.

Fond thanks to Barb and Jim Ferguson for your quiet and unquestionable support behind the scenes. Barb, I wish you were here.

Juggling clients, a business, a family, and my bike racing would not have been possible without the timesaving brilliance of my talented editor, Michael Levin. Thank you for guiding me on this crazy adventure, pulling out of me what I didn't know was there, and delivering me to a destination more incredible than I thought possible. You're a gift.

Only writers can really understand the pains and 'hair-pulling frustration' of writing. What began as a coincidental pairing of writing partners in a book-writing program developed into a deep friendship. Thanks, David Fields, for all your harebrained ideas, for challenging my thinking and going far beyond the call of duty. You're incredible.

To Dana Ben Halim and Wendy Burch-Jones, my incredible business managers over the years who just took care of 'the other stuff' and helped create space to focus, my gratitude.

I'm not a big fan of boxing, but I liken a coach to the support team a boxer is greeted by between rounds. The bell rings. That little stool appears magically in the corner of the ring, the boxer sits down, often exhausted, and whatever is needed to get back in the ring is provided: stitches, strategy, water, a kick in the butt, encouragement, you name it. To my coaches, past and present, who have contributed knowingly or not to this project: Cindy Barlow, Chris Barrow, Ken Abrams, Faith Hoy, Glenn Estrabillo, Howard Chan, Jennifer Kroezen, and Sarah Kapoor. Thank you for your unrelenting stand for what's possible.

The main difference between a coach and a good Mastermind group is that in a Mastermind group, they gang up on you! A deep thanks to Mastermind group members past and present for the no-holds barred, no B.S. support over the years that culminated in this project: Steve Marsh, Jennifer Allen, Gillian Todd-Messinger, Mel Thompson, Paul Copcutt, Doug Emerson, Andrew Finklestein,

Jayme Dill-Broudy, Jennifer Koretsky, Sandra De Freitas, Sital Ruparelia, Michael Margolis, Stephan Doering, Bill Metcalf, Joanne Goodrich . . .

. . . and especially my riding partner, fellow Masterminder, bike guru, stalwart friend, and all-around inspiration, Derek MacNeil. You're a rock star, bro.

To my many incredible clients who've taught me more than I've taught you. A special thanks to Cathy Honor and Janette Watt. You've believed in this company from the very beginning, and together we've transformed lives and leaders. It's been a remarkable ride and you've made the journey unforgettable, thank you.

To the unbelievably talented colleagues, clients, friends, and just darn-right great people who gave me their time and wisdom when I knocked on their doors researching this project: Carolyn Burke, Bruce Burrows, Margo McConvey, Sue Usher, Sherry Duffy, Myra Rosen, Michael Sasarman, Michael Spence, Steve Rosen, Paul Fortin, Paddi Riopelle, John Arnott, Naomi Shaw, Sam Hayes, Louise Mitchell, Patrick Rodmell, John Eggen, Linda Duxbury, Nick Thadaney, Rajiv Silgardo, Colleen Moorehead, Dan Chornous, Jan van der Hoop, Laura Garton, Jim Davies, Stephanie Willson, Dr. Chris Twigge-Molecey, John Pearson, Esther Auger, Janice Hampton, Thomas Wilson, Maja Dettbarn, Mark Stein, Helena Gottschling, Michael Bungay Stanier, Jennifer Pierce, Myra Rosen, Jude Fairweather, and especially Maureen Jillain for our Friday night phone calls! You're all a clear reminder that the genius is in the collective; thank you for sharing yours.

To all of you, this isn't my book, it's ours. Thank you for who you are in the world.

The difference between what we do
and what we are capable of doing
would suffice to solve
most of the world's problems.

—Mohandas K. Gandhi

Author's Note

Why I'm Passionate About Emerging Leaders

Have you ever heard the saying that the worst students later make the best teachers?

It's often because they have spent so much time trying to figure out how to make things work. They have made all the mistakes in the book, they've struggled, and they have also cheated in every way imaginable. They figured out every short-cut to get around things, to avoid things, and to make things easier. As teachers, these experiences help them to see when their own students are running up against the same challenges. They make great teachers—not only from the sense of having learned a lot, but also because they can see where others can get tripped up. They can identify where other people are struggling.

That's been the case for me in this area of leadership and particularly "emerging leadership" as I define it in this book. While I've got the business degree, the adult education certification, a coaching designation and endless training as a professional coach, the greatest learnings came from the School of Hard-Knocks. I was the worst student of leadership for as long as you can possibly imagine. Indeed, my lack of leadership first showed up when I was five years old. It was the afternoon before Bobby's Halloween party, and my dad and I were making the greatest Halloween costume ever created. I was going to be a yellow duck. That's right, a yellow duck—made out of cardboard.

Now, no parents in their right minds would ever dress their child up as a cardboard yellow duck. Or maybe as a child, you had a cardboard costume, too! The cardboard pieces are strapped around your shoulders and the boards chafe your legs as you walk, and using the washroom is nearly impossible. A big wind comes up and it folds and you keep taping it together—that was the yellow duck costume.

So, the afternoon before the party, my dad and I worked together, cutting, stapling, having a real father-son bonding experience. It was great. While we were doing this, I remember feeling a knot in my stomach. But I was having so much fun with my dad, I just ignored it. We kept on working away, and when we were finished with this big yellow thing, we placed it on the coffee table. Picture a little five-year-old boy looking up at the coffee table with a large cardboard yellow duck on it. I remember thinking, 'Wow. This thing is amazing; I will have the best outfit at the party!' But in that exact moment, I finally realized what the knot in my stomach was about. I was terrified of standing out. What if I went to the party and everyone laughed their heads off at me? What if they thought I looked funny? What if my friends wouldn't talk to me and thought I was silly?

When it came time to actually go to the party, I was all dressed up as the duck—beak and everything. My proud father was taking pictures and then said, "Okay, Jamie, time to go to the party." But I couldn't go. I stayed home. I just couldn't face what might happen. That event was the first bookend of over twenty years of me playing my life really, really safe.

During that twenty years I was the shyest kid in class. Girls absolutely terrified me. I had no idea what to say to them, what to do with them. Not only that, when I finally started dating when I was seventeen, I stayed in my first relationship for seven years. Why would I do that? So I didn't have to date again!

I took the safe degree at university: I got a business degree because it's marketable. After I graduated from University in 1991, I traveled the world for a little bit, and then returned home to the job I thought I wanted: the blue-chip job. The safe job. While I was there, people recognized my potential. And I was doing some pretty cool projects, but still playing it really safe—doing enough to look good, but still staying in control. I wouldn't take chances, I would conveniently avoid the big stretch projects, or I would only do very few of them, because I was scared to go to the party. Frankly, I was scared of screwing up.

I'd met April in my final year of my degree in 1990. I remember shortly after we began dating writing a letter to my brother describing her as a red Maserati. Remember letters before e-mail? At the time, I wasn't feeling very good about myself—not sure where I'd go after school. We were in a recession. I felt like an old VW bug chugging along in the slow lane of life, and the red Maserati just went whipping by me in the fast lane. She had this great red hair. She was a varsity athlete and had tons of friends. She was a recognized student leader—everything—a phenomenal human being. I wondered why the hell she was with me. In 1994 we got engaged.

A week before we were to be married in 1995, she was almost killed in a car crash.

She was actually going to our wedding photographer on her bicycle and she got hit by a car. She was air-lifted by helicopter to St. Michael's Hospital in Toronto and her parents were told that she probably wasn't going to survive the flight. She was unconscious and remained in a coma for twenty-eight days. How long a person remains unconscious is indicative of how much damage has been done to the brain. When someone goes into a coma, the body shuts everything unnecessary down, so it can heal the brain. Once the brain is healed, it begins to turn the body back on.

On our first planned wedding day, April was unconscious and horizontal in the ICU with tubes up her nose. Her body moved in random ways as she lay there. My relatives were coming in from the US and the UK for our wedding. It was the most surreal and terrifying experience you could imagine—waiting for her to "wake up." When she emerged, we had to start all over again. Like, *all over* again. I helped her learn to tie her shoes, I taught her how to walk. I changed her diapers. Her weight had dropped from 130 pounds to 110 and she suffered from hemi paresis, the paralysis of the right half of her body. She had severe memory loss and didn't even remember our engagement. She had what is known as retrograde amnesia, and she lost an entire four years of our relationship, obviously along with other memories. In the end, she spent five years in rehabilitation, from 1995 to 2000.

Within six weeks of the crash, she was just learning how to walk again while at the hospital. I had to go back to work because I just couldn't afford to not be there. But I visited her every night. One night, I walked into her room, where she was supposed to be confined to her bed—but she wasn't there. I asked her roommate where she was, but she didn't know. I went to the nursing station. They didn't know where she was.

I had that sinking, panicking feeling that all parents who temporarily lose, or think they have lost, their children at a park or large public space know all too well. Oh, no—where is she? Nobody knew the answer. I went running down the hallway, checking everybody's rooms, not caring about privacy. I just went in looking for her. When I got to the end of the hall, I hadn't found her. I went out the exit door, out to the stairwell, to go down the stairs, and I stopped in my tracks...

There was April—one-hundred-and-ten-pound April, in her hospital gown, holding on to the railing of the stairwell with her functional left arm. She was climbing up those stairs, part supporting herself on the railing, part hopping up, pausing, helping her right leg to follow, supporting herself again, hopping, helping her right leg . . . she was determined to get better and *nothing* was going to stop her.

She had every reason and excuse to be sitting in bed doing nothing—doctor's orders. But she was going to get better no matter what *anyone* said. While she appeared frail and weak, this was the strongest person I'd ever met. In that moment, I saw what leadership was all about. It's not about looking good. It's about truly going after what you want in life. Contrast the kid in the duck suit, wearing the perfect outfit, who still wouldn't go to the party—and the gal with the unflattering hospital gown and frail body, who was going no matter what. That was April. At that moment I knew my Maserati was back. That experience on the stairs was the other bookend of my twenty years of playing my life safe.

And that's why I do my business.

Emerging Leaders haven't been "out there." They don't have years of experience to rest on. They don't know if their ideas are going to fly or not, or if they're going to totally bomb, or cave, or what their senior leaders will think. They're a little like me in that yellow duck outfit, feeling confident that they'll have the best costume at the party...and then feeling unsure about whether to go to the party at all.

They say cancer, or a serious accident, brings clarity. All of a sudden, I knew what was important to me. It was about getting out of the mindset of playing it safe, playing small, playing not to lose.

April and I married a year later and she's now the mother of our two children. Her rehabilitation results have been phenomenal. I've got a framed article and photo from the *Globe and Mail*, one of our national newspapers here in Canada, about her recovery and how we managed it. We were featured in the Focus section, a full feature with big pictures. We've also been on CBC Radio, Breakfast Television, and all kinds of other media.

April was the one who inspired the beginning of Footprint Leadership. She was the catalyst, the model—the incredible human being. And that is why this book is dedicated to her.

What I had been missing before April's accident, and what's been so fabulous about our partnership, is that it has set the context for my work. It's not just a nice, warm, fuzzy story. Instead, it symbolizes the stand I take for Emerging Leaders. Because that's who I was. I was the guy who had ideas, dreams, and potential (like we all do) but wasn't sure how or if to use them. On the outside, I looked like I had it all together and was producing decent results; but on the inside, I struggled. I got in my own way.

With the clarity and resolve April's crash brought me, I emerged from my own shell and learned to truly unlock my potential and swing out. And that's what I offer those I work with: the tools and opportunity to unlock what's possible. I empower them to truly bring their skills, talents, and leadership to their lives, their work, their company—and indeed, the world.

The world is a wonderful, yet crazy place.

And we need *you* more than ever.

It's time for us all to put on our yellow duck suits . . . go to our own party . . . and have the time of our lives.

Introduction

Who Are the Emerging Leaders in Your Organization?

To answer this question, we must first define leadership. Seth Godin said it best:

"Leadership is not management. Management is about utilizing known resources most effectively to get a defined job done. Management is all about efficiency. Burger King hires managers. **Leadership, on the other hand, is about creating change that you believe in.** Leaders have followers. Managers have employees. Managers make widgets. Leaders make change."

"Embracing change" has become a cliché. It's merely the ante to get into the game of business today. Seeing what's needed and making change happen is the new predictor of leadership success. Act or be acted on.

Emerging Leaders (ELs) are people whose abilities to make change—that they believe in—is developing, coming into existence, and coming forth into view or notice.

Leaders can and do "emerge" at any time. I'm not suggesting they don't. ELs' talents typically emerge and begin to be recognized in the form of much greater responsibility between the ages of thirty and forty-five. During this period, the EL's career exploration and experimentation phase, which was so characteristic of their twenties, is replaced with a clearer sense of personal strengths and what's important to them professionally. This clarity is also compounded with a greater sense of personal responsibility, which often arrives in the form of mortgage payments, children, and other important personal interests that develop when ELs begin families. If it's not families, there are an untold number of personal passions ELs make a point of exploring. The interests run the gamut from hiking to cycling, from band practice to online gaming, from volunteering with a local charity to taking extensive trips abroad. Involvement can range from casual interest to full out commitment. Some of it requires specialized (and not inexpensive) equipment; all of it requires time.

They are thirsty for the challenges and opportunities that will help them grow, yet they have strong demands outside of work as well. They may even reach senior *roles* during this period, albeit with far less experience than *established* senior leaders.

In a way, Emerging Leaders are the perfect opportunity and paradox for organizations: They're reaching a point in their lives where they have a greater sense of professional direction and personal responsibility, but at the same time, they're still a relatively clean slate in terms of their leadership behaviours. Their professional habits are still malleable. This adds up to engagement, focus, growing skill, and a willingness to learn from past results without being limited by them. It's a unique, formative, and incredibly influential developmental period for most leaders, and a tremendous opportunity for employers to shape and leverage their most valuable assets.

They are your company's next generation of leaders. The market forces I'm about to outline demonstrate that these Emerging Leaders are needed more now than ever before.

For over a decade my company has specialized in building the future leaders of organizations. I've worked with thousands of Emerging Leaders and have an intimate understanding of what makes them tick. In this book, I will share with you the guidance I offer the *established* Senior Leaders—or SLs, as I usually refer to them throughout this book—to identify, train, leverage, and retain the next generation of leaders in their organizations: the Emerging Leaders in their midst.

Section I

Inside the Heads of ELs

1

Climbing Mt. Everest

It's 4:55 p.m. on Friday evening. There's a huge project you wanted to get out the door *tonight,* and you suddenly realize that the two people in charge of it are heading out the door.

One is wearing tennis sneakers and is headed for the gym.

The other is headed for his son's T-ball game.

The next generation of leaders—the Emerging Leaders upon whom you rely to keep your company competitive and successful—can be a mystery at best, and at worst, a disappointment or a huge HR problem. Or maybe they're all three of those things at once. These employees seem unpredictable, are harder to manage, and their priorities are difficult to gauge. Half the time, they don't even seem as *serious* about work as you've grown to expect.

Oh, they want to make money, rise rapidly through the ranks, and get the most exciting projects to work on. But there's something hard to understand about the next generation of leaders. Practically every senior manager realizes at one time or another, especially when an important deadline rolls around and the younger leaders are clocking out as five p.m. approaches, "They're not like me."

They *aren't* like you. Those employees coming up behind you work differently, live differently, think differently, expect differently, and in every important way, march to the beat of a different drummer.

This can drive bosses crazy. It's a source of endless frustration and concern to senior managers, and the issue isn't just theoretical. Senior Leaders must identify the next generation of leaders, and motivate and incent them properly so that they will want to stay and, in time, become Senior Leaders themselves. There's the rub: how do you identify which of your employees are worthy of the investment of time, money and energy it will take to lead on a bigger level?

How do you trust people you don't quite understand?

Every Senior Leader was once a fresh-faced and eager-eyed Emerging Leader. And although it may seem difficult when you're facing a full plate of responsibilities and priorities, fully leveraging your Emerging Leaders will require you to pause—and get into their world. To put it simply, your next generation of leaders is a different breed. They can be just as hard-working as you, and you've seen them step up to the plate when it's really necessary. But at the same time, they have other priorities, other draws on their time and energy, which hold just as much, or perhaps even more, sway as their professional ambitions. They often don't think the same way you do about work, money, life, marriage, parenting, or anything that you hold dear. More often than not, they aren't willing to put in long hours at the office, to sacrifice nights and weekends for the cause, to wait their turn, to remain silent in meetings, to defer to office politics—in short, to do many of the things that you had to do to reach the top. How do you understand these employees' priorities—and get them to understand yours?

The Path to the Peak

Ever thought about climbing Mt. Everest? In some ways, it might be easier to reach the top of the world's highest peak than to understand, identify, motivate, train, and retain your most promising future leaders. At least with Mt. Everest, you can hire guides, buy oxygen tanks, train properly, and follow in the footsteps of those who have gone before you. When it comes to working with your Emerging Leaders, typically those people in their thirties and early forties who are moving up in your organization, there are no guides—at least, not until now. The purpose of this book is to share with you insights about how your Emerging Leaders—your ELs, as we will refer to them in this book—think. We will examine how they think about themselves, about you, about work, about life, and what you need to do in order to generate the most value together.

If you're climbing Mt. Everest, as you rise up from Advance Base Camp, you will come to a series of deep breaks in the path to the top called crevasses. The crevasses are deep, and falling into one is almost inevitably fatal. The only way to traverse the crevasses and keep on the path to the top is by crawling across ladders, which are fastened to the ground by experienced Sherpas—and by not looking down! Think of me as your Sherpa to help you cross the crevasse that separates your understanding of the world from that of your ELs. There's a yawning gap between the way you think and the way your ELs think. This book is intended as a ladder to bridge that gap. It offers a successful approach to the peak; however, no two climbers make their way to the top in exactly the same footsteps. There are infinite ways to make this journey your own.

Climbing Mt. Everest and succeeding in business have a lot in common. You've got to be careful where you step, and you've got to be careful about whom you choose to put on your team. If the people coming up behind you aren't capable and experienced, you can pay an extremely heavy price. You're literally harnessed together as you make the ascent, so you have to have as much confidence in those behind you as they have in you.

I've worked almost exclusively with Emerging Leaders in mid- to large-size companies, and I've helped their Senior Leaders, SLs like you, maximize the value of their Emerging Leaders, those who are coming up the mountain behind them. I want to share with you in this book the insights that I have learned from working with the *established* Senior Leaders—typically individuals in their mid to late forties, fifties, and sixties—and the next generation of leaders. It's my intention that this book will make you hundreds of thousands or even millions of dollars, in terms of talent leveraged, productivity gained, and misunderstandings avoided.

The Looming Leadership Void Ahead

The Senior Leader may not be entirely happy with the attitude or perceived work ethic that their Emerging Leaders have. But they have an even bigger problem to face: demographics. In the business world, there is an unavoidable and growing leadership void that stems from two root issues:

1. The mass of baby boomers who are reaching retirement age and will soon leave the workforce, and
2. The lack of skilled workers entering the workforce.

Here's a brief—and troubling—picture of what the changing landscape looks like.

There simply aren't enough people entering the workforce as Baby Boomers retire. The US Bureau of the Census projects that in the US, "Almost 90 percent of the next decade's [2000–2010] net increase in the working-age population will occur in the fifty-five to sixty-four year age category."[1] The Conference Board of

1. William B.P. Robson, *Aging Populations and the Workforce: Challenges for Employers* (Winnipeg: British-North American Committee, 2001), 7.

Canada, which extensively studies the nation's labour trends, states that "[the] steep decline in labour force growth is at the root of the labour supply crisis that will develop in Canada around 2010."[2] Indeed, the study forecasts a shortage of one million workers in Canada by 2020, stating, "[The] dimensions of the problem are enormous, and the growing difficulty in hiring or retaining existing employees will dramatically alter the structure of the Canadian labour markets."

A survey by global management company Accenture of more than 850 top executives from the US, UK, Italy, France, Germany, Spain, Japan, and China found that two-thirds of executives put the inability to attract and retain talent second only to competition as their key threat to business success. Similarly, a survey of 1,350 European executives from twenty-seven countries conducted by The Boston Consulting Group and the European Association of Personnel Management (EAPM) concluded that managing talent is the most critical challenge facing businesses today. In fact, 72 percent of executives believe that human capital has an impact on innovation and new product development; 82 percent believe that human capital has an impact on profitability; and 92 percent believe that it has a significant effect on customer satisfaction.

A US Conference Board study done in 2004 determined that 65 percent of the companies surveyed reported that talent management had become "dramatically or considerably more important" since 2001.[3]

A survey by SEI's Center for Corporate Futures (Wharton School of the University of Pennsylvania) in 2007 uncovered a concern that "difficulties in finding, retaining, and growing talent" was the number one priority for international business respondents. What's also interesting is that their choice was picked from

---

2. Conference Board of Canada, "Charting a Canadian Course in North America," in *Performance and Potential 2001–2002* (Ottawa, 2001), 55.
3. Lynn Morton, *Integrated and Integrative Talent Management: A Strategic HR Framework*, Research Report 1345-04-RR (New York: The Conference Board, 2004)

a list of challenges that included the growing influence of India and China on business.[4]

A 2007 research report, *Leadership 2021,* found that 81 percent of US companies are concerned that their supply of leadership talent will affect their future business plans.[5]

But not only is the labour market declining from the top down, it's also creating a gap that will need to be filled. According to a year-long study conducted by McKinsey & Co., over the next fifteen years there will be 15 percent fewer Americans in the thirty-five to forty-five year age range than there are today. Assuming that the US economy averages 3 to 4 percent growth each year, the demand for thirty-five to forty-five-year-olds will jump by 25 percent, even as the supply will be plunging by 15 percent.[6]

The reality is, the senior generation of leadership, the Baby Boomers, have begun to hit retirement age. When they retire, they will create a yawning gap in management—at the top, where the losses will be most keenly felt. It's a business cliché that your most valuable assets take the elevator to street level every night, but it's a reality. Businesses have mostly paid lip service to this inevitable reality. In 2004, an International Public Management Association for Human Resources (IPMA-HR) survey of employers discovered that 63 percent of respondents did no workforce planning of any kind. A 2003 study by the Society for Human Resource Management (SHRM) of their entire membership base found that 60 percent of the members had no succession planning in place in any form.

Many Senior Leaders are just beginning to see and act on the threat that this demographic shift implies. As your senior leaders

---

4. Matthew Guthridge, Asmus B. Komm, and Emily Lawson, "The People Problem in Talent Management," *McKinsey Quarterly*, no.2, 2006.
5. Leadership 2021, Research Report, Corporate University Xchange, Harrisburg, PA, 2007, p.4
6. Charles Fishman, "The War for Talent," *Fast Company* no. 16 (1998), http://www.fastcompany.com/magazine/16/mckinsey.html.

leave, the transfer of power, responsibility, and leadership begins. Are you ready?

Got Depth?

Progressive organizations measure their leadership capacity not by the leaders they have today but by how many people in their organization could step up and fill leadership positions *tomorrow*. In other words, they measure their "bench strength," just like any basketball team. Why is this so important? Companies have profit and growth opportunities that they can only bring home if they have the personnel on board.

Does your business have the bench strength? Are you hiring, retaining, and training Emerging Leaders sufficiently to meet opportunities today and possibilities tomorrow? If you're not, you're not alone. But imagine the consequences of retaining incapable people in major roles for extended periods of time. The losses inherent in your company's resultant failure to respond to market opportunities could be incalculable. When the crunch hits, everyone, from senior management to the customers, feels the pain. And world markets are less forgiving than ever before. With the substantial variety of significant variables at play today, your ability to build strength for the future is not a luxury; it is a requirement for survival.

I use the term "bench strength" because the players on the court right now are your Senior Leaders. The people on the bench are your ELs. You might have five Michael Jordans, but unless they can play at full intensity for forty-eight minutes, a team with lesser superstars and a strong bench is likely to beat the five Jordans every time. The guys with the bench will always win, because they can simply exhaust the competition. So the questions Senior Leaders have to confront are these:

How many people do we have who could replace our current key leaders?

What's the quality of the replacements, and how capable are they?

If you've got only one Emerging Leader per department, you don't have enough bench strength. What if that replacement leaves? What if that person gets recruited by your San Francisco office? Now what do you do? Here's the reality: the EL, especially an EL confident of his or her value to an organization, is far more likely to jump ship than were employees in the generation of today's Senior Leaders. SLs often operate from a mentality that you pretty much work for one company for your whole career, or if you change jobs, it's a big deal, and you might only do it two, maybe three, times in your lifetime. ELs are a little more like Goldilocks—if one situation doesn't feel right, they'll move to another, and then another, and then another. A résumé with a lot of job changes was a badge of dishonour even a few decades ago. It meant that you were unstable, that you couldn't commit. ELs have no such compunction about keeping their résumés neat and tidy. And a résumé littered with a half-dozen jobs in a decade is no sign of instability, in their minds. In this day and age, having multiple jobs on a résumé is less a sign of instability and more a representation of one's mobility, flexibility, and a desire to find the best possible situation. If you look at an EL's résumé and don't like his or her prior mobility, then you are not right for him/her. This is a 180-degree difference from prior generations, who had the mentality that they needed to craft themselves, their experiences, and their résumés to please the potential boss.

So maintaining an anemic bench is a serious gamble. Lack of bench strength limits your ability to take on your initiatives, and provides far less flexibility to respond to market pressures or opportunities. There are simply not enough people to draw upon who have already developed leadership qualities. It all adds up to less bench strength and, therefore, less flexibility in organizations.

Just as sports teams sometimes throw unseasoned rookies into a game, corporate enterprises are finding it increasingly necessary to throw untested individuals who haven't yet grown into their full maturity as business leaders, into extremely demanding situations. This forced compromise arises from not only the demographic reality but also from the fact that, while organizations are getting flatter, *jobs* are actually getting bigger. At Pepsi, in the 1980s, the average age of an executive was forty-two. Now it is thirty-one. Can you imagine a wet-behind-the-ears thirty-one-year-old doing the job of someone who previously had eleven more years of leadership experience?

Younger people are getting bigger jobs sooner, and this has a significant impact on organizations. All of this makes it more imperative than ever to identify and develop the individuals within your organization who have the greatest potential to stay, to lead, and to make meaningful contributions. When we develop Emerging Leaders effectively, and in the right numbers, we've got the bench strength to handle problems and opportunities now. We can handle defections, both internal and to our competitors.

Time to Hit the Ground Running

Today's ELs are different from SLs. The looming reality is that the future of your organization and what you've built will rest upon them. If today's ELs are understood, embraced, invested in, leveraged, and retained, your business is going to thrive. Those savvy companies that see this will be poised for long-term growth and sustainability. The laggards, the ones who are trying to develop their future leaders over a period of twenty years, as they did in the old days, are going to be dinosaurs. You can't afford to wait that long. The meteor is coming, disguised as demographics. And we all know what happened to the dinosaurs.

So here you are, an SL, trapped by the rising expectations of the marketplace, tight limitations on what you can spend on head count, and a new generation of ELs who are less focused on your best interests than they are on their own futures. How do you get the most out of these individuals? How do you stay competitive with a workforce seemingly so unstable and hard to read? How do you cross that crevasse that separates your mentality from theirs?

Luckily enough, doing all of this is not as difficult or strenuous as it may seem. It requires engaging your Emerging Leaders in new ways and training them well enough to take their own initiative rather than shackling them with antiquated approaches and dragging them along. You'll reap the benefits multifold, and you'll be surprised to find that the process is better than painless—it's rewarding.

So let's get started.

2

Your ELs' Frustrating Little Habits

A generation ago, it was simple to manage people: "This is the task, this is what you do, so go and do it."

That's so last century.

ELs can drive SLs crazy. ELs usually want the plush projects, the dreamy jobs that SLs like you worked forever to get. SLs tell me all the time, "Never in my career did I get these kinds of opportunities at that young an age, or that early in my career, as these people are expecting." In other words, your ELs want the exciting, fun projects, but the grunt work still needs to be done, and it often appears that they just can't be bothered with it.

It's frustrating, because with their drive and enthusiasm, ELs are great at tackling these cool, fun projects. But when it comes to final implementation and getting things complete—the boring stuff that has to be done to generate value—either they don't want to do it or they're already onto the next project. SLs sense in ELs a tendency toward entitlement, a belief that they should only do high-level work and never have to focus on aspects of a job they find boring. In fact, SLs frequently report that their ELs' attitudes border on arrogance.

At the same time, it's taking longer to find good people to fill positions. In the past, an SL could put out a job listing or run it through Human Resources and get an avalanche of résumés from which to pick and choose. Today, tons of résumés are still coming in, but most SLs today realize that there are fewer really good people to hire. Finding the fit is taking longer and longer. One SL told me that it takes eighteen months to two years to fill an important position. That's an eternity when you're trying to run a business. It also means that you've got fewer people trying to do more and more work, and the work that has to be done somehow feels beneath the dignity of the ELs you're expecting to do it. This is most definitely not to say that many ELs aren't willing to pitch in—over the short term, they often do. But eventually, their different set of priorities dictates that they should be out the door at five o'clock for that T-ball game. Nerves get frayed. Deadlines get pushed back. More stuff falls between the cracks. The quality of the work changes.

SLs frequently tell me, "When I look at the best people on my team, one of the things that they want is more opportunities to grow by doing interesting projects." You can understand that impetus; you've always wanted to have opportunities for growth as well. That's why you've gotten where you are. But you were able to wait for these opportunities, or seek them out diplomatically. Somehow, many ELs come off as bucking at the gate for projects that they may not be ready for, and they start making requests under circumstances in which you, in their shoes, would almost certainly choose to bide your time.

Many Senior Leaders find it bothersome that ELs are so straightforward in terms of asking for what they want, both in terms of time flexibility and also in terms of asking for the projects that interest them the most. SLs find it especially irksome that ELs just seem to want it all . . . yesterday, before they're entitled to it. The SL says, "I had to work my butt off to get to where I am now, and some young whippersnapper wants to do the same kind of projects it took me fifteen or twenty years to get to. Who do they think they are? They don't have the business sense and they don't have the business maturity! It just doesn't work that way!"

This appearance of EL entitlement is exacerbated by the current business climate. The challenge right now is that organizations are under increasing pressure to eliminate inefficiencies. They're cutting out layers of decision-making—middle management—that can get in the way or slow processes down. The result of this streamlining is flatter and flatter business structures: there is less opportunity for promotion than in the past, because there are fewer positions in the hierarchy. So ELs are either competing for positions that don't exist, or they're getting promoted much further in one step, because all the middle ground has vanished.

Everybody always talks about what a great thing it is to get rid of middle management. However, getting rid of middle management limits upward mobility, which may result in not being able to provide much incentive for ELs. The question really becomes, how do I provide my ELs with opportunities to grow and learn when an organization is flat?

ELs Speak a Different Language

SLs tell me, "Promoting people is the least of my problems! I don't even know how to begin *communicating* with them!"

That's true—many SLs don't know how to communicate effectively with their ELs. It's not like the old days, where the command-and-control model that many senior leaders were "raised" in professionally was more commonly accepted as way to get things done. Leading this next group of leaders, this new generation rising up, is different. Part of crossing that crevasse is finding the most effective ways to communicate with ELs. Senior Leaders traditionally were more political in terms of how they communicated with their bosses. They got to where they are by being prudent in terms of what they said to whom. ELs are more straightforward about what's going on, which means that SLs are often much more politically savvy than those reporting to them.

What comes as a surprise to many Senior Leaders is that the Emerging Leaders often don't even *care* about walking that fine, political line. Who is most politically sensitive in today's business climate? The SLs. If a Senior Leader wanted to work on a particular project, he would pull the right strings, go through the right channels, and follow the appropriate process for making that happen. ELs have less time, interest, or patience for the political process that has traditionally existed in enterprises. If an EL wants a project, they'll be far more assertive in asking for it directly. They'll often just say what they think. ELs tend to be less consensus-driven than their leaders. The ELs may not always be thinking outside the box, but they are almost always thinking outside the organization chart.

There is a certain level of maturity in the business world that can only be obtained over time. One way this lack of maturity in ELs can show up is when an EL is invited to a senior meeting. Perhaps the Emerging Leader has been invited to talk about a project she's working on. In years gone by, the Emerging Leader would only speak about the particular topic she was invited to discuss and would remain silent for the rest of the meeting. Yet sometimes Emerging Leaders will arrive and start participating in the rest of the meeting as if they were at the same level as the other participants. This inevitably bewilders some Senior Leaders, who wonder how ELs have the effrontery to speak up. The Senior Leader would never have done that when *she* was coming up! So how can this younger generation?

The ELs' tendency to speak up and speak out comes from a number of factors. First, ELs tend to be much more result-oriented in their work. Process or rules of procedure are much less important than the results they accomplish. Therefore, ELs often get frustrated with consensus-focused meetings, which are held to allow team members to discuss projects in detail. They want to cut to the chase—and they may very well speak up in the middle of a conversation if they feel it has gotten circuitous or beside the point.

Another reason why ELs may appear to SLs to be speaking out of turn is that high-performing ELs seem to want attention to a much greater degree than SLs did earlier in their careers. They're driven by a need to remain marketable, and they know the best way to do this is to first produce results and then talk about them.

Let's say there are ten people on an operating committee and three out of four of them are potential Emerging Leaders. Then there's the Senior Leader responsible for this operating committee. The SL thinks he's going to run the meeting on his terms. Instead, the three ELs seek some time to discuss their projects, accomplishments, and needs. Of course, it doesn't *always* work this way because some ELs are more reserved. But many Emerging Leaders create a perception among the Senior Leaders that they need attention and that they're even immature, in the sense that they're constantly vying to look good. In the past, the politically savvy approach to "getting ahead" often looked like quietly participating in meetings so as not to risk embarrassment by saying something stupid.

It's not that that culture has gone away, because office politics will exist as long as there are offices. In the cultures of some enterprises, office politics remain particularly rampant. This is especially true where particular managers are stuck in the old command-and-control way of doing business. However, Emerging Leaders are less and less willing to allow politics to determine their behaviour. And so, while politics still exist and need to be managed, they have much less patience for it.

At the same time, I've encountered many Emerging Leaders who do just the opposite: they tow the line so much that they hesitate to contribute. Confounding as it may seem, you may find that some of your ELs simply remain unbelievably quiet, rather than storming the meeting, beating on their chests like apes, and trying to take control of the environment.

What many SLs don't realize is that both of these challenging tendencies—either to speak too much or to speak up too little—come from the same tendency of this age group. ELs are operating from a standpoint that we'll discuss in great detail over the course of this book. I call it Me, Inc. They see themselves as working for their own tiny company, comprised of one employee: themselves. Me, Inc. is like a small business that enters into a working relationship with your business. The goals of your business are important, but your EL will always be answerable to Me, Inc. first and foremost. We'll talk about this more in chapter 4, but for the time being, the important thing to realize is that your Emerging Leader is going to behave in ways that he or she believes will produce and prove more value for Me, Inc. This might mean overzealousness or it might mean reticence. Either approach often appears unsavvy from the SL perspective.

Two questions arise: how much do they have to conform to your way of thinking and how much do you have to conform to theirs? The important thing is that a spirit of partnership should prevail. The SL no longer holds all of the power, giving them the right to dictate everything to the ELs. Conversely, the ELs need to see the value that the SL brings to the table in terms of experience, wisdom, and institutional history. There's going to be give and take. For reasons we'll discuss, ELs simply will not work on the same basis that you did at an earlier point in your career. It's just not going to happen. But even accepting the fact that they won't do everything the way it's been done in the past, how do you find the time to train them to understand what your way represents?

ELs Need Time That You Don't Have

Given the demands most SLs face, the number of fires they have to put out, the number of crises they have to work through, and the flattening of organizations that can have them doing more detailed work at levels lower than them—anything that is not immediately revenue-generating tends to fall by the wayside. Chief among these "important but not urgent" tasks is the business of developing the future leaders of your organization. All too often, this focus goes by the boards when customers are screaming one thing or suppliers are screaming another. Engaging and then developing the right people is often a task that drops off the to-do list entirely.

As we've introduced earlier, given the current demographic reality, it's not a task that organizations can avoid anymore. Organizations that fail to engage, train, and develop Emerging Leaders do so at their peril. But an even worse scenario is when Emerging Leaders rise up into new positions of authority . . . but don't have the training and skills they need to succeed. Or when they see themselves stagnating with your organization, not being given opportunities to learn, and you lose them entirely to companies that *are* offering training and opportunities to grow. If we aren't setting people up to do great things, we are inevitably committing them to fail—or cut bait. So one of the key topics we'll discuss is how to grow your Emerging Leaders faster while *simultaneously* delivering value and addressing the fast and furious needs of your business (a serious downfall of many leadership development programs in my opinion).

ELs Seem Underprepared for Delegation

This leads directly into the question of delegating—or, to put it more bluntly, *releasing*—tasks. Hesitancy to delegate is natural. An SL has to feel confident that an EL can actually take on a project or initiative and make it succeed. How do you release your responsibilities to a younger or less-seasoned employee with confidence that he will be able to take the project on and make it work? We'll talk about the best ways to prepare Emerging Leaders, in order to ensure that those projects and initiatives will happen on time, the way they're supposed to happen. The other part of this equation is SLs having the courage to give ELs the opportunity to succeed . . . or to fail and learn from failure.

Contrast the way a company like Google handles delegation. At Google, up to 20 percent of an individual's time can be spent on his or her own projects. This gives Google employees the initiative to create some cool idea and then go and play with that idea. Google people can form teams, devote a lot of time, energy, and resources to a project, and totally screw it up . . . but *it doesn't matter.* It could be a runaway success, which would be terrific, but even if it fails, there's virtually no downside. There's little risk to the company, because the project was never a revenue source for the company in the first place. Google simply gives its employees the opportunity to be kids in the candy store, trying whatever they want, with no consequences should they fail. Of course, not all organizations have the luxury of Google's particular breed of flexibility and cash reserves, but their approach speaks to their mindset about innovation and creating an environment that fosters it.

The ability to try, fail, and not suffer for one's failure is sadly lacking in most organizations. In most workplaces, *everything* is big and significant. If you fail, then you're tarnished. How does an EL get that next opportunity once he's failed? How can he get a raise? At talent-review time, when it boils down to deciding who's on the "top-talent list," ironically enough, those who displayed initiative to take appropriate risks and failed—the very people on whom you should be betting the future of the company—can be the ones less likely to make the cut.

Concern about "career-limiting moves" and internally tarnishing one's reputation can be one of the biggest factors that paralyze new ideas and stagnate leadership growth for ELs and SLs alike. Senior Leaders can have great influence on encouraging appropriate risk-taking in ELs—if they themselves can embrace this attitude as well.

ELs Want to Do It All on Their Own

In today's business world, you can't manage the way you were managed.

As we alluded to earlier, many Senior Leaders were raised in the command-and-control model that preceded them. In fact, the organizational culture of North America was founded on the hierarchical approach of command-and-control management. In this model, the focus was on compliance with authority, with few questions asked. Many SLs were "raised" in this world professionally, and although they often prefer a collaborative approach, it's natural to manage the way you were managed. Of course, like any behaviour, there are degrees to which it is expressed. But ELs simply don't speak the command-and-control language, and for those SLs who prefer this style, you'll likely have found that this approach falls on deaf ears.

SLs often find it absolutely maddening that ELs tend to work so independently. They don't want to be told what to do. They don't want to have someone looking over their shoulder. They don't want to have a bunch of "check-ins," where they are responsible for demonstrating whatever progress they have made. Instead, what they want to hear from you, the Senior Leader, is this: "Here's a project, and here's what we want to accomplish. Make it happen." And that's it.

In the past, a dominant theme in the lives of current SLs was micromanagement. The bosses of the SLs managed them very closely. It might have looked like, "Here's a project, and here are the thirty-eight steps we're going to follow in order to complete the project. Go do these thirty-eight steps." That's the command-and-control model. In the beginning of your career, when you were tasked with part of a project, you might never even have been told about the whole scope of the project. You were likely given your own small piece of the puzzle, and you were expected to take care of it in keeping with the more traditional, controlled management approach that dominated business for so long.

ELs, on the other hand, want to know the big picture. They want to see the project in its entirety, partly because they need to know that they're contributing to something greater than themselves, but mostly because they don't like being micromanaged. As for the thirty-eight steps to completing the project, they're not interested. Their attitude is not, "Give me step one and step two this week, and next week you can give me steps three and four." They want to figure out the thirty-eight steps by themselves. This need for independence conflicts with the desires of many SLs to control the project (the way they were), to know what's going on, to be kept very informed, and to be able to make changes. The EL wants more autonomy, but many SLs prefer greater control. The truth: ELs *do* want to collaborate, but in their book, this does not involve being told what to do.

Furthermore, unlike a number of SLs, ELs respect skills and competence more than seniority. To them, there is nothing worse than working for an incompetent manager. So the fact that you're an SL will not automatically garner you your EL's respect. This can be a frustrating reality for many SLs, who aren't particularly eager to have to prove themselves to their younger employees, when proving themselves is exactly what they've spent their entire careers doing with those above them. The result: tension, which could be avoided. There are ways to resolve this seemingly impossible split. And we'll talk about how to do that further on in the book.

ELs Just Aren't Like You

Senior Leaders are often looking for people like themselves to hire, mentor, and promote—but when it comes to ELs, SLs find there is something unfamiliar about them. It's human nature that we're most comfortable when we're surrounded by people that are like us. A generation or two ago, the world, and certainly the business world, was much more homogenous. White men hired other white men, especially those who came from the same schools, backgrounds, and even families. Values were the same from one generation to the next. It was easy to find people just like yourself.

And then the world changed, and with it, the workplace became more democratized. The world went from Lawrence Welk to World music without missing a beat. But this new heterogeny in the workplace leaves the traditional manager at something of a loss. How do you find people "just like you" when the category of "just like you" has all but gone away? The senior leaders often need to recognize that looking for people just like themselves isn't necessarily a good solution, for several reasons. First, there aren't that many of you left! And second, we need people who have fresh eyes that can look at today's complex problems and offer new perspectives. But that's not enough. We need those contrary perceptions to be shared and heard. The days of being surrounded by "yes" people, where decisions and thinking were rarely challenged, won't help Senior Leaders to keep up with the pace of today's change. Abraham Lincoln was admired for surrounding himself with people who challenged his thinking. This strength is also one being attributed to US President Barack Obama for making choices such as Hillary Clinton as Secretary of State.

Emerging Leaders, by virtue of the smaller number of years they've been on the job, lack the information and history the Senior Leaders have. But my viewpoint is that this is actually positive. The Emerging Leader brings fresh eyes and a new perspective to situations that SLs aren't always capable of bringing. Granted, ELs may have less maturity when it comes to how to handle certain situations or how to approach certain things, including conflict in the boardroom or any other form of dispute resolution. But the value of the fresh perspective that an EL brings should not be discounted just because he or she doesn't "look or act like me" or lacks the Senior Leader's experience.

Often, it is difficult to acknowledge or recognize an EL's fresh perspective because of the differences in communication styles between ELs and SLs that we discussed earlier. A Senior Leader may have been in the organization for twenty-plus years, or may have held the senior vice president position for some time—but that experience can actually blind her to fresh thinking and new ideas. So when an Emerging Leader brings out a new idea, she may be so startled by the EL's outspoken style that she doesn't even hear the idea for what it is. The SL's first thought may not be, "Will it work?" but "Who the hell are you?"

To compound matters, if the idea is a good one, then suddenly the Senior Leader looks bad to himself and maybe to everyone else in the meeting. You've been here *this long* and you haven't thought about *this* yet? It certainly isn't from lack of intelligence or competence. But again, fresh eyes and approaches can stir things up. Sometimes it's tough for the Senior Leader to get his ego out of the way and allow the Emerging Leader's ideas to receive due consideration, especially if they have been communicated in the assertive way described above. It can be threatening when someone else comes up with new ideas that the Senior Leader hasn't considered before. It's likely that a considerable portion of your ELs work under SLs like the one I've just described.

The truth is that if we don't understand others, it's easy to find fault in their behaviour—both for SLs and ELs alike. We're all well aware of this tendency; it's human nature. But actually getting a reign on it and keeping it from obstructing our paths to success is a more difficult and complex task than you might expect. Despite appearances, impasses between Senior Leaders and Emerging Leaders are rarely caused by bad attitudes on either side. Instead, individuals get tripped up on their misunderstanding of the other's motivations. So let me show you the inner workings of your ELs and dispel the misunderstandings that may get in the way of clear communication and a highly rewarding relationship with them. Who exactly are your Emerging Leaders? What's on their minds? What are they striving for, and why? Let's meet your typical ELs and identify their motivations and priorities, which SLs might not be aware of.

3

A Day in the Life of the Emerging Leader

Typically, Senior Leaders have always *organized their lives around work.*

By contrast, Emerging Leaders *arrange work around the rest of their lives.* And their lives are often very complicated, indeed.

As society changes and gender roles blur, more women are moving up through the ranks in organizations, often balancing motherhood and career, and more men are taking increasing responsibility in their families' lives. The notions of Mom's Café and Mom's Taxi are becoming relics. These days, Dad is driving carpool, too, and he's changing diapers, and fixing meals, and his company car may have one or more booster seats in the back.

At the same time, Emerging Leaders have taken the "work hard, play hard" mentality to new extremes, building their weekends around family activities, sporting events or other interests. Not as much company golf for this cohort. Or they might be passionately committed to volunteering or some other "hobby" (often more like a second career, in their minds)—writing, painting, hiking, collecting art, you name it. Big races or big gallery openings mean a big commitment to training or time, so both male and female Emerging Leaders are balancing work, child-raising obligations, demanding fitness routines, social commitments—and oh, by the way, relationships and marriages, when they can squeeze it in.

This is important information for Senior Leaders to take in, because it demonstrates how radically the world has changed in just a generation or so. The stay-at-home mom concept is no longer feasible economically for most families, and an increasing number of women are unwilling to stay home when they could be competing in the workplace. All of this makes for long, complicated days for Emerging Leaders, who are attempting this extremely difficult multi-level balancing act. It also means that there is less time or bandwidth available in their lives for the thing that used to be the far-and-away number one priority for many Senior Leaders: namely, work.

So if you're wondering why your Emerging Leader doesn't get in until nine in the morning, it's because he's on his exercise bike, driving carpool, or changing diapers because his wife has already left for her job. If you're wondering why that same EL expects to leave the office by 5 or 6 p.m., it's because his daughter has a soccer game he wants to attend. He may or may not check his Blackberry while he is there. And if you're expecting your EL to work this weekend, well, there might be a little bit of a conflict. She's been training for a half iron-man triathlon for the past eight months and in her mind, it's just too much for you to ask her to forgo that race. And by the way, it's in Phoenix, so don't expect her to be available by phone for much of the weekend, because she'll be on planes Friday night and Sunday afternoon. She'll squeeze in some "Blackberry Work" here and there in airport lounges, if it can work with her schedule.

In short, back in the day, when your boss asked you to jump, you asked, "How high?"

When you ask your Emerging Leader to jump, the response is, "How come?"

Remember, Emerging Leaders *organize their work around their lives, not the other way around.*

Buckle Your Seatbelt . . .

Let's see exactly what ELs are doing when they're not at the office.

If you've never been the hands-on parent in the morning, getting the kids off to school—either because you never had children, or more likely, because your spouse was taking care of these matters while you were off on your early morning commute to work—it's a bigger, harder job than you ever might have imagined. You've got to get the kids' lunches ready. But here's the challenge: there's nothing your kids want to eat. Madison likes bologna, Liam likes pickles, and Devlin throws up every time he smells mustard. Or is it Liam who throws up? You can't afford to get it wrong. So you're juggling the mustard jar in one hand, a Sponge Bob Squarepants lunchbox in the other (is it Madison or Liam's?), while Devlin tugs at your pant leg because he just spilled his Cheerios in his lap. You're also trying to keep one eye on the dog, who's scratching desperately at the back door and probably on the verge of having an accident—but at the same time, you have to call up the stairs for the third time to Liam, who always needs an extra twenty minutes to roll out of bed.

Finally, you get Devlin cleaned up and give him a fresh bowl of cereal (with rice milk, not real milk, because you're pretty sure he's the one who's lactose intolerant—or is it Madison?). In the meantime, Madison, miraculously, is in her coat and good to go . . . but Liam's only just now stumbling bleary-eyed down the stairs, and he's as good as gone. So, you have to make a last-ditch effort to get Liam's cowlick to lie flat on his head, open the back door to let the dog back in with your left hand while you grab the three lunches with your right hand. And just when you think you can head for the door, you remember they've all got to put their shoes on. Madison can tie her shoes like a pro now, but Devlin's got his left shoe velcroed to his right and Liam's not even thinking about shoes yet—he wants another glass of orange juice. Somewhere, in the back of your mind, you remember that the Anderson file has to be put together before 9:30 a.m., and for a brief moment of pre-coffee madness, you wonder if you'll be able to read it at the stoplights between the kids' school and your office. Then the dog barks, bringing you back to reality, and somehow, through some strange combination of luck and parental voodoo, you manage to get all the lunches, shoes, homework, children, and of course, your Blackberry out the door and into the car just under the wire . . . and then Madison calls from the backseat, "Daddy, I have to pee!"

Why do I mention all of this? To give you some sense of the stress that your Emerging Leader has experienced by the time he or she finally makes it to the office, right around that 9 o'clock hour. When you were an EL, your biggest stress was the traffic, or that your train was running late. For today's EL, the stress levels are endless and varied. They say good things come in small packages. Well, so do multiple crises, if those small packages are your kids.

After exercising, and then getting exercised over the insanity of a typical preschool morning with kids, your Emerging Leader certainly hasn't had a lot of time to get his or her game face on. There's not a lot of time to decompress, of course, because by nine o'clock, your Emerging Leader's inbox is jammed, her cell phone is full and can't accept messages, text messages are piling up, and she hasn't even begun to think about her own proactive agenda for the day. As a country song put it, "I'm always running, and always running behind." And that's on a good day, when all of the children are healthy and there aren't *that many* Cheerios all over the floor. What if the school had called a snow day? That would spark the impromptu spousal debate over who's more available to take the day off and watch the kids: who has more vacation time saved up, whose project can be completed from home, whose boss is more understanding, whose job is more important. The EL's life is a constant balancing act, and when you've got that many plates in the air at once, the slightest misstep throws the whole show off kilter.

Of course, not all ELs have families. But that's not to say that your single ELs aren't being pulled in twenty directions at once, too. They're the ones who are likely to have the fitness regimens of Olympians, or who are gunning to get a short story published in that up-and-coming ezine, or who are balancing their volunteer commitments as a Big Brother or Sister or spending time restoring that '91 Miata. Or maybe they were out the evening before on their fifth disappointing blind date in a month, so they're trying to catch up on work in the wee hours of the morning before rushing into the office. ELs of today have a myriad and endless stream of interests and commitments outside of work.

Remember that old tagline for Army ads? "We do more before breakfast than most people do in a day." Your Emerging Leader would hear that expression and say, "They're singing my song."

Compartmentalization Is for the Lucky Ones

Now the actual workday begins. Believe it or not, for many ELs, stepping into the office feels like a reprieve. It's not that they see your company as a place to escape and slack off; it's just that they can start expending their energies in a different way, and often, compared to the frenetic rhythm of their outside lives, the office pace actually feels *easier*. Unfortunately for them (and for you), compartmentalization is no longer possible in our communication age. Just as ELs often manage their work life during their personal time, they often need to manage their personal life during their work time. Their lives are so expansive and jam-packed that it's impossible to keep things from bleeding into each other.

Did you take calls from your spouse when you were starting

off, no matter what the setting? Your Emerging Leader often will. It might be good for the relationship, but it certainly doesn't do much for the ELs' work focus; at least, that's how many SLs view things. Many other Senior Leaders simply aren't aware that their Emerging Leaders are taking phone calls during the workday from spouses, handling domestic crises, negotiating who's going to handle carpool later that afternoon, trading in favours, or simply haggling over whose workload this afternoon is really less important than the other person's and therefore can be safely postponed without too much risk to deliverables, reputation, or career. Who blinks last?

Finally, the Emerging Leader gets focused on work (assuming that the children's school doesn't call with the news that "Liam got hurt on the playground, won't stop crying, and is insisting that you, and not your spouse, come get him"). The stress never abates because the Emerging Leader has one eye on his computer screen and as the afternoon passes, all too quickly, one eye on the clock.

A quarter to five rolls around and that's when the Emerging Leader starts downloading work to his laptop to take home to be done that evening. Why doesn't he stay to do it? Because five o'clock is his exercise time, and if he doesn't get to the gym right then, he most likely won't for the rest of the evening. The gym is the sacred ground, the holy place, the temple of the gods for the Emerging Leader—and attendance, in his mind, is mandatory. He's *got* to work out, and he's got to work out at five, because if he leaves the gym at six he can just make it home by six thirty, when the nanny or babysitter has to leave. Now comes family dinner, which is usually just as frenetic and challenging as the breakfast hour, but with the added complication that everybody's exhausted and cranky.

Getting the kids to bed without major fighting, time-outs, or embarrassing behaviour on the part of the parents is nothing short of a miracle, and everybody in the family knows it. So they get back from all the sports activities and get the kids into their bedtime routine. He reads the smaller children a story. Before he knows it, the kids are nudging him: "Dad! Wake up and keep reading!" It gets to the point where he can't even fall asleep unless he's holding a copy of *Dr. Seuss* or *Curious George*.

At nine p.m. the kids are finally down, including the one who couldn't fall asleep, and now it's time to open the laptop and start doing the work downloaded earlier that day. That's why Senior Leaders receive all these e-mails that are time-stamped midnight, or even later. He works until midnight, and his spouse is in another part of the house, pounding away on her laptop, and by the time they fall into bed, they have barely said a word to each other the whole day that doesn't have to do with crisis management, child management, or who's going to remember to buy more toilet paper and lightbulbs. One of them is inevitably sound asleep by the time the other gets there, so it hasn't exactly been a stellar day in the history of the relationship. But what are they going to do? Nothing. Just set the alarm for six a.m., grind five and a half hours of sleep, and do the whole thing over again the next day.

Many Senior Leaders, when confronted with the reality of what their Emerging Leaders' days are truly like, shake their heads in dismay; they often want to go and give their Emerging Leaders a hug and a bottle of NoDoz. Actually, many Senior Leaders find the scenario I just sketched out to be alarming and even disturbing. How could anyone expect to put in a meaningful day at the office, to take on greater responsibility, to close deals, to stay focused—or even just to stay awake—with all these circus-like distractions going on? It was easier a generation ago, when people working their way up the org chart could count on their spouses to handle all of these home and child-raising issues. Often, when I paint this picture of the EL's life for Senior Leaders, they say they didn't realize how good they'd had it, or how relatively uncomplicated their lives were. Back then, all you had to focus on was your career—getting the work done and occasionally making some allowances for office politics. You can see why your Emerging Leaders don't have time for office politics. They barely have time for *anything*.

What can you, as a Senior Leader, do? You can't turn back the hands of time to the way things were in the '80s or the '70s or the '60s. It would be nice if you could staff an office with people who had the exact same work ethic and priority set as you. But, unfortunately, the reality is that your pool of future leaders comes from a generation with different needs, perspectives, and priorities. As we'll discuss in the next chapter, when the corporate world disavowed its bond of lifetime loyalty to employees through the downsizings of the early '80s and '90s, it created the situation that exists in today's world in which Emerging Leaders put the concept of life balance ahead of career and income. Actually, ELs desire the same kind of rewards that you earned, but they are not prepared to sacrifice. They just don't have that time to offer.

This is the reality of the Emerging Leader's day—insanity in the morning and insanity in the evening, bracketing a jam-packed day in the office. Yes, they're more often willing to work that extra eleven p.m. to two a.m. shift, but how long can they keep that up without some costs to their health, their marriage, or their family? Not forever.

So if you're a Senior Leader and this is the lifestyle of the people you manage, what alternatives do you have to tearing your hair out, retiring on the spot, or going crazy? On top of that, there's a lot that the ELs don't want SLs to know . . . about who they are, what they want, and what they think about you and your company.

Understanding the Emerging Leader's thinking is your key to engaging and leveraging ELs. To risk gross oversimplification, it's different from yours! It's also the subject of our next chapter.

4

What Your Emerging Leaders Do Not Want You to Know

Senior Leaders and Emerging Leaders are often playing separate games with different rules and even different objectives—but your Emerging Leaders don't want you to know it. They want to appear as if they're on the same playing field as you, passing the ball in the same direction. In actuality, they're slowly trying to edge that ball onto a different field entirely, a field where they can define what's out of bounds and where the goal line lies. *What they don't realize, however, is that their game could be compatible with yours, and there's no reason why you can't share the field and win together.* The first step to making this a reality is to take a look at the cards they play close to their chest. We'll look at each of these individually, but here's an overview to start with:

1. I'm Loyal to Me, Inc.—First and Foremost
2. Boss, You Have More Power Than You Know
3. Seniority Means Nothing
4. I'm Not as Confident as I Appear to Be
5. I Won't Sacrifice the Way You Did, Mr. SL
6. I Often Take Calls from Headhunters and the Competition
7. I'd Work for Less Money If . . .

I'm Loyal to Me, Inc.–First and Foremost

The main thing your Emerging Leaders do not want you to know is that they do not work for you. They work for themselves. They saw the loyalty their parents—usually their fathers, or friends of their fathers—gave their employers, and they saw that loyalty go on unrecognized, unrewarded, and seemingly disregarded in the downsizings of the early '80s and early '90s. They do not want to risk the same thing happening to them. So, although your enterprise may be their nominal employer, in fact, they are primarily loyal to a company they call "Me, Inc."

Me, Inc. is a professional services business that hires itself out to an employer without any expectation that the relationship will last forever or until retirement comes. A Me, Inc. employee is not interested in the gold watch, the pension, or the ceremony honouring fifty or twenty-five or even ten years of devotion to the company. The Me, Inc. employee—which is pretty much every Emerging Leader—believes that the business world is not looking out for his or her interests so they have to watch out for them themselves.

Your EL does not want you to know that. Your EL wants you to think that he is a happy employee, that he is a loyal employee who will run through walls for you—as long as running through that wall does not conflict with anything else on his calendar. He wants you to believe that he feels the same way about the company as you do. But in his heart, he does not, and he never will.

For ELs, it is no longer about climbing the corporate ladder. Instead, it is about climbing the professional ladder. Since companies have flattened, it is more difficult to climb up the hierarchy, or as Robert Townsend's 1970 bestselling book's title says go *Up the Organization.* Some ELs do have a goal of rising up in your organization, in point of fact, but they are not counting on that corporate ladder always being there for them. They know that ladder could be yanked out from underneath them at any time. They have seen it happen to their parents, to their peers, and to themselves!

You might have sought to move up the rungs of authority and recognition, as previous generations of employees did before you. But today, your EL, operating as a Me, Inc., knows that the title is no longer a measure of job security. Instead, paradoxically, job security for an EL does not mean that he can count on a long-term career with the organization. *Instead, job security for an EL means remaining marketable.* If the organization is not promising to take care of them over the long haul, they have to take care of themselves. They are not really employees—they are independent professional services firms, and they provide their own specific services to your organization for as long as you both find it a good fit.

If a Me, Inc. is a business, then it faces the same needs as any other business—it has to get business to stay in business. That's why remaining marketable, and increasing one's marketability, is so important to an EL. In the past, some companies used the job transfer strategy to ensure that an employee's primary loyalty was to the organization and not to the surrounding community. By transferring managers to a new locale every three years or so, a company could work to ensure that it, and not an outside community, was the primary source of stability in an employee's life. In theory, the employees were learning about a new facet of the business, but in reality, they were transferring their primary loyalty to their employer and not to a neighbourhood, a school system, or a set of friends. Today, it is much harder to get an EL to move simply for the company's sake. If an EL is going to move, or do anything, they must see that next step as something that will increase their marketability or fit into their life plan, not just help them move up the ladder with their current employer.

How does a business get business and stay in business? Its assets and capabilities must be attractive to potential clients. The same is true for your Me, Inc.-focused ELs. They know that what attracts employers are individuals with really great skill sets and great experiences under their belts. They know that their next employer will be looking at them in terms of these questions: Will they bring value to the organization? Will they bring experience, knowledge and skills?

So if you want to get the most out of your ELs, it's crucial to view them from the same perspective that they view themselves—individual Me, Inc.'s who want work experience that will create tangible value and that will make them more marketable to the next employer outside *or within their current company.* You might not like the idea that their focus is not so much on you as it is on the job after you. But that is the reality, and if you want the most from them, and if you want them to stay with you for as long you would like them to, you have to provide them with the experiences and opportunities that will allow them to develop the skills and knowledge base that will be attractive not just to your organization, but to your competitors, as well.

In a sense, it's counterintuitive: *groom your ELs to leave you.* The beauty of it is, if you are successful in training your ELs, they'll stay with you longer because you are satisfying any need they might have that would make them look elsewhere. On the other hand, if you disregard employee development, they'll move on to an employer better able to help Me, Inc. grow into the best personal services business it can be. Hatch, an international engineering and consulting firm, is a perfect example of success in this balancing act. They identified five key drivers for retaining employees:

1. Creating a climate of lifelong learning.
2. Offering a share in the company ownership.

3. Encouraging a culture of excellence and innovation that employees want to identify with and belong to.
4. Providing challenging work.
5. Offering the opportunity for global travel.

Hatch is so committed to these five drivers that, not only are their employees more likely to stay on board, but those that do leave them often quickly return. Their employee relations policy addresses the EL's desire to constantly expand the breadth and depth of Me, Inc.—their life goals outside of work—so that it is capable of putting better and better services on the market.

In short, your Emerging Leaders' primary sense of responsibility is not to you; rather, it is to themselves. By grooming them to leave, you actually give them fewer and fewer reasons to go.

Boss, You Have More Power Than You Know

As a manager and a Senior Leader, you are the single most important person in your ELs' picture of the company hierarchy—period. You have more impact on their company loyalty than any other single factor. In fact, ELs see you as the gatekeeper to their future professional success, the growth and development of Me, Inc. It's like they're looking at the org chart in a fun house mirror, and you end up stretched out of proportion, towering over the rest of the organization. In the early years of your career, you might have grown accustomed to being hyper-aware of the company hierarchy and staying in bounds with regard to the chain of command. Your ELs know this about you. They understand that you interpret loyalty as a sense of connection to your team, your department, and the organization as a whole. ELs do not want you to know that their worldview is 180 degrees different. The EL's secret is that, in his eyes, he's working for a company of two: himself and you.

You have influence on which cross-functional projects your

ELs are entrusted with, what opportunities they're exposed to, and what kind of promotions they ultimately receive. So, when it comes to hierarchy, their focus is on you: how you treat them, how you relate to them, and what interest you take in their development. They want to create a mutually beneficial relationship in which both of you can collaborate and win. They want to give you great results and exceed expectations—but they want development opportunities and challenging work experiences in return. While the trade currency of the relationship is "development for results," the outcome is loyalty. Indeed, ELs can be fiercely loyal to great managers, often following them around the organization as they move from department to department.

This means that you have an extremely important role in determining whether the EL reporting to you will stay with your organization. That is because they're most responsible and loyal to the manager, not the organization as a whole. We'll discuss later how the culture of an organization may be crucial in attracting a new EL. But when it comes to retention, the immediate manager will always trump culture. If a manager is unpleasant to work for, the EL is not likely to stay just because he is working for a popular brand. *People leave managers; they do not leave companies.* If an EL is working for a poor manager in a great company, they are much more likely to leave than if they were working for a great manager in a poor company. This is the case because the manager always has the greatest impact on the day-to-day work experience of an EL and what opportunities are made available to him or her.

Now here's the catch: ELs want to look good in front of you, not just because they want you to be pleased with their job performance, but because you hold the key to growth opportunities. This means that they do not want to look stupid in front of you, and they may be reluctant to admit mistakes. Let's be honest—this is hardly a generational characteristic. It naturally arises in the boss-employee dynamic. But it's certainly something to be particularly aware of with ELs, because the stakes are so high for them to create the most marketable Me, Inc. they can. ELs do not want to have conversations with you which reveal weaknesses or areas in which they are not confident. This has huge implications for any SL running a business. No matter how great a manager you think you are—and I've worked with countless ELs reporting to great SLs—you will never get the full picture from your ELs. You will never know everything you need to know about the people you are managing or the situations they face.

Seniority Means Nothing

One of the greatest changes between the generation of SLs in the workplace and the generation of ELs is that ELs really do not care how long their seniors have been at the same company. They do not care how long you have been working. That is too old-school for them. They do not care because sticking around the same job smacks of the old loyalty paradigm, which they do not buy into. In the world of the ELs, loyalty no longer exists—it is more about: Can you do the job? Are you a competent manager? Can you take care of me? That is what impresses them—an SL who "gets it," who understands that the EL's need for balance and flexibility is different from her boss' need to work.

ELs live in a world where their peers, or even people a decade younger, are creating companies like Facebook and YouTube while writing code at the corner Starbucks. Their role models and corporate heroes are twenty-something gazillionaires who had an idea, cranked out the code, got a lot of attention on the internet, and took the whole thing public.

In the minds of ELs, being proud of years of loyalty to the same organization is like being proud of driving a Buick. ELs do not think about Buicks. They think about Ferraris. In their minds, they *are* Ferraris. They want to go around the track at 200 miles per hour. They do not want to line up in the pits for twenty years for an opportunity to set a new speed record. That is how they think.

I'm Not as Confident as I Appear to Be

Despite all the assuredness they display, however, ELs are not as confident as they would like you to think. And this is yet another thing they do not want you to know about themselves. They come to your organization with different ideas, different ways of doing things, a fresh perspective. But their relative inexperience means that they lack the confidence to look foolish, to fail. They may not be automatically impressed by the fact that you have been working for the same organization for ten to twenty years, but they are impressed by your confidence and your track record. You have been around the block, and they have not, and they know it. So it is important for you as a Senior Leader to see past the seeming self-assuredness and recognize that your ELs are often "fronting"—they are pretending to be something they know they are not. This is a phenomenon I've uncovered time and again in my experience coaching ELs. I see so often the remarkable, innovative ideas that ELs are capable of—and their reticence to bring them forward. A huge part of my job in working with them is to encourage them to take the risk of bringing that value to the table.

What does this mean in practical terms for an SL? Understand that your ELs want to create win-win relationships with great managers with whom they have a deeper level of trust, respect, and partnership. If you are committed to help them grow more, both as your personal philosophy and as organizational policy, they will reciprocate in spades.

I Won't Sacrifice the Way You Did, Mr. SL

Although you are more important to your ELs than the company as a whole, and they may look at your accomplishments with starry eyes, they aren't prepared to sacrifice the way you might have. Their loyalty to you and their work is tempered by their commitment to the rest of their lives. They have a "work-to-live" mentality as opposed to a "live-to-work" mentality that many SLs adopted. They view the rest of their lives—their social lives, their marriages or relationships, their families, and their extracurricular activities—as far more important than work. They saw the price their parents' marriages and families paid for the often single-minded focus that the previous generation put on work. They do not want to pay that price—not with their families, not with their spouses, and not with themselves. You matter, the work matters, but having a life outside of work as well matters even more. Do they want you to know that? Of course not—you control their opportunities. They're trying to get both: opportunities and balance.

I Often Take Calls from Headhunters and the Competition

Your ELs seem to have taken the challenge in John F. Kennedy's inaugural address and stood it on its head. In their minds it is, "Ask not what I can do for the company. Instead, ask what the company can do for me." In an EL's perfect world, she has the opportunity to do work she enjoys, provide value to the organization, and build her résumé at the same time. She does not want the organization to know she is building her résumé, but since she has no reason to believe that the organization will be there forever for her, she also has a limited sense of obligation to the organization for any great length of time.

SLs sometimes suspect that the foregoing is true. But how do you deal with it? As an SL, you're responsible for the immediate goals of your department or division. Perhaps you'd like to give your ELs opportunities to grow, but grow where? What if they want to move on from your department to bigger things? Perhaps they would like your job or would want to leave the organization altogether. In any scenario, it likely means short-term pain for you. This tension between the short-term needs of the business (and the SL) and the growth needs of the EL can set off an unspoken dance in which the Senior Leader pretends to honour the requests for growth opportunities and the EL feigns loyalty and commitment. In reality, the EL is increasingly open to other opportunities. ELs will take calls from your competitors and from headhunters—and believe me, for your ELs, the call frequency is increasing. I can't tell you the number of times I've had confidential conversations with ELs, getting them to seriously consider their options and have more proactive conversations with their supervisors instead of jumping ship prematurely. They continually have their eyes on the horizon of what is out there for them. Remember, in the EL's world, marketability equals security. And we all gravitate toward security.

I'd Work for Less Money If . . .

If your ELs "work to live" and are constantly seeking to create balance between their professional and personal lives, nothing is more precious to them than time. They are changing diapers, carpooling kids or running marathons in their off hours, which often means they have less time and attention to give to their work. Does this mean that you should screen out well-rounded job applicants in favour of those who seem to have no life outside of work? Good luck finding them! At the same time, however, consider the fact that your fully-rounded Emerging Leaders may have the ability to get a lot more done because they have become more efficient by nature of the multiple demands on their limited time. A client once told me, "I would hire a qualified single mother over a university student any time, because that person has to prioritize things in her life." In other words, that single mother has to be extremely efficient and effective, or she will be in deep trouble. It is those people with time pressure, because they have fuller lives, who bring a greater sense of efficiency to their work day. As the old expression goes, if you want something done, give it to a busy person.

Because time flexibility is so important to ELs, they would be willing to trade money for more freedom in terms of scheduling their personal time. Once again, this is something they do not want you to know, because when it comes right down to it, they want both the money and the flexibility—who wouldn't? But they are willing to work for less money if you give them more flexibility. They place time freedom at such a premium that they will trade dollars for it. What's a key way to engage your ELs? Give them the flexibility and time freedom they need to train for their marathons, to be home for the six-o'clock baby feeding, or for whatever rocks their world.

This may go beyond the day-to-day sense of "I have to leave early because of my son's tee ball game." Perhaps your EL is starting a family and wants extended maternity—or even paternity—leave. Your EL wants to know that yours is the kind of organization where the job will still be there when the baby is old enough for daycare. It can be difficult for organizations to provide this kind of flexibility, but if yours does not, someone else's will, and your ELs will gravitate towards employers who are mindful of their needs. Which employers allow you to cut down your hours so you can train for Ironman? Which employers will give a father time off to bond with his new child? This information is out there and is easily obtained by your internet-savvy ELs. The organization no longer exists in a vacuum, and you are competing for the best of the ELs every single day. They might not want to take a whole year off, but they just do not want to work sixty or seventy hours a week when they have a young family—or a major race to train for. The only way to tiptoe through this minefield is to partner with your EL as opposed to the traditional mindset that says that the employer owns the employee's time. That old model will not work in today's world. We'll talk more about that in section 3 of the book.

Senior Leaders can find it frustrating to have employees who routinely take off for doctor's visits, workouts, school plays, or any other reason that would have been unacceptable in the workplace a generation ago. Many SLs are used to having more structured environments, and often equate the flexibility that ELs crave with a lack of commitment or contribution. Often, in an SL's ideal world, the EL sits at his desk all day long and gets work done, like a clerk in a Dickens novel. But your ELs do not have time for Dickens novels. They are too busy on the StairMaster or reading their small children bedtime stories. This is why SLs have to get used to the fact that ELs do a chunk of their work in the middle of the night. When you see e-mail from your EL date stamped 1:27a.m., he did not start his computer to put that time stamp on it in order to impress you. That was when he finished his work!

Productivity no longer means sitting at a desk all day long. It means getting work done whenever, wherever. It can mean working from home, telecommuting, working in the local coffee shop, working at different times of the day every day, and all kinds of different options. Sometimes my SLs wish that they could simply trade in their ELs with this hypermodern approach to time, work, and productivity for different ELs who go about things the traditional way. The problem, of course, is that the pool from which you can gather replacements will be just as time-stressed as your current people. So you might as well make the best of the people you've already got.

The place to start is by recognizing that your EL's relationship to time doesn't come from a sense of entitlement, although it may appear so. I've known some SLs who resent the fact that their employees believe they have the freedom to come and go as they please, to go out of the office when they see fit, to work in the middle of the night, to abandon their desk for a coffee shop because they like the ambience there instead of in their cubicle. But these tendencies don't come from a lack of work ethic. In actuality, they come from a flexible and efficient nature born of years of juggling multiple obligations.

As far as the EL is concerned, he is not doing anything wrong. He is accomplishing the projects you gave him, right? So what if he is doing it at one thirty in the morning instead of one thirty in the afternoon? He does not believe in face time, in sticking around the office just because the boss has not gone home yet. Typically, if the boss is an SL, the boss is going home last.

Well, What's *Not* Secret?

So what do ELs want you to know about them? They are go-getters, do-what-it-takes kind of people; they want to learn. They want to be engaged. They are fully engaged with the rest of their lives, and they would like their work lives to be just as stimulating and growth-oriented. They want that not just because they have high expectations about life in general, but because, as we saw a moment ago, the more engaged they are at your place of employment and the more skills they are building, the more marketable they can be internally and externally.

They are bright and they are energetic. They have to be energetic, because high energy is so deeply linked to being fully-engaged in life. They are ambitious. They want to have interesting, challenging careers, as long as they do not conflict too greatly with their personal priorities. They just want to have great lives. ELs do not say, "I'll do what I really want when I retire." They refuse to take on that attitude. Instead, they want to have a great work life and a great life outside of work as well. They want to be present for their children in ways that their parents might not have had the opportunity to be. They think back on their fathers and they say, "He provided everything we really needed, but he was just not around." They don't want to follow in those footsteps.

In addition, they are motivated by big goals—as long as they feel that they are an important part of achieving those goals, and not just simply a cog in a machine. They have zero tolerance for that sort of thing. They are less interested in face time or acting political in the workplace—they are driven more by results. That is because they have far less time for political manoeuvring. They have too much else going on in their lives. They come to work each day looking not just for success or recognition or a paycheck. They are looking for meaning. Meet their needs, and they will meet yours.

Summary: Senior Leader/Emerging Leader Comparison Table

	SENIOR LEADERS (ESTABLISHED)	EMERGING LEADERS
GENERAL DESCRIPTION	**Ability to produce results is well developed and fully recognized by the organization** Typically holds senior positions in the organization. Extensive tenure, experience or track record of results.	**Ability to produce results is coming into existence and beginning to be formally recognized by the organization** Growing responsibility; may or may not hold a senior role. Shorter track record of results and/or inconsistent results.
DEMOGRAPHICS	Usually > 45 years of age. If > 55 years of age – likely a single-income household. Their children are out on their own or needing less time.	Often 30-45 years of age. Usually dual career, dual income households. Young children with higher time/energy needs and/or have strong interests outside of work.
GUIDING WORK/LIFE PHILOSOPHY	**Live to work** Life needs to fit in with my work/career comitments.	**Work to live** Work commitments need to fit into my life.
MOTIVATED BY/ LOYAL TO	**The Company, My Career** "I work for and serve an employer." Doing a good job = Security. Career and income focus.	**Me, Inc.** "I am a business." Marketability = Security. Whole life and balance focus.
STYLE OF WORK	**Structured** People-focused. Likes to work in teams. Cautious about change. Politically savvy.	**Flexible** Results-focused. Prefers to work independently with little supervision. Opportunistic about change. Straightforward and direct.
RELATIONSHIP TO AUTHORITY	**Challenges authority** Likes flat and democratic organizations. "I want to prove what I can do for you."	**Not impressed by authority** Respects competency and skills, not seniority. "Tell me what you will do for me."

Section II

Who Are the ELs in Your Company? Identification and Selection

5

Do You Buy 'em or Grow 'em?

The term that defines today's era in sports is "free agency." No longer does one player stay with an entire team for his whole career. Instead, a player might be drafted by one organization, reach the major leagues of his sport in a second, attain stardom in a third, and finish his career with a fourth team. The concept of long-term loyalty to a team in sports is just as much of a relic as the concept of long-term loyalty in business. It brings to mind Jerry Seinfeld's comment about being a sports fan: "Everything changes. The players change, the coaches change, the managers change, the owners change. The only thing that stays the same is the uniform. You're rooting for . . . laundry!"

General managers of sports teams, therefore, find themselves with the vexing challenge of trying to predict which athletes in their farm systems are likely to become major leaguers, which players on other teams are worth trading for, and which free agents are worth paying exorbitant salaries in hopes of winning right now. As a senior leader in the business world, your position is almost identical. You've got players coming up the ranks in your organization. You've got to make bets on the future of each of these individuals, and you have to do so with limited information. How a player performs in the minor leagues is not always indicative of what will happen when he reaches the majors.

There's also the question of whether to grow your own superstars or acquire them from other organizations. The future of your organization is riding on your ability to recognize top talent. You could be world class at training people, but if they don't possess the fundamentals that will allow them to become superstars on your team, all the training in the world won't make a difference. So in this chapter, I'm going to discuss the topic of how to identify which of your Emerging Leaders are worthy of the time, energy, and attention it takes to grow them into the big contributors you need them to be. And since business, just like sports, lives in a world of free agency, how do you pick the ones who will stay long enough in your organization to make a contribution that justifies the time and effort it takes to train them?

In the past, an athlete spent his entire career with one team. Today, in the era of free agency, everything is different. Most players spend no more than three or four years with a given team. A team might win the Stanley Cup or the Super Bowl and then all the players' prices go up. Other teams start poaching your players, and the team itself can go from "we to me." So even after just a few winning seasons, a team has to rebuild again. Sports teams today are in a phase of continual rebuilding as the players' commitment to particular teams themselves diminishes. The same is true in business. In the past, a senior leader might have been with the same organization for twenty years, and might never expect to leave that organization until retirement. To the SL, the shorter the résumé, the more respectable you are. To an EL, the longer the résumé, the broader your background and experience—and therefore, the more employable you will be. So we're looking at diametrically opposed world views.

In a world where players will likely stay with the team for

shorter periods of time, what do you do as an SL? Do you play the free agent game? Or do you develop a farm system and hope your new recruits stay long enough to put the training you give them to good use? It's a good question: the question of whether to buy talent or grow it.

Transfer the Employee—But Will His Success Come Along for the Ride?

How many times have you seen it happen that a team in any sport trades for a star player, and pays him a sizable salary and bonus to make the move, only to discover that the player cannot duplicate his prior success with his new team? In sports, it seems as though that happens more often than the opposite: a player who catches fire with his new team and rises to even greater heights. Most often, by the time a player reaches free agency status, his payday is in front of him, but his best playing days are behind him. So this is a situation to be avoided.

The same thing is true not just of players, but of coaches. Glenn Rowe, of the Richard Ivey School of Business, University of Western Ontario, studied this impact of context on the ability of leaders to create results. To do this, he examined the success rates of NHL Stanley Cup-winning Coaches and General Managers. Of the 289 coaches that had worked in the league since 1917, only twenty-four won the cup more than once, and a meager three of those were able to do it on more than one team. Only one of the General Managers during the same period won a cup with more than one team.

Buying talent, whether we're talking about a player or a coach, often leads to expensive failure and disappointment. The overwhelming experience in business is that buying talent—often expensive talent—is no guarantor of success. Just as coaches find it extremely difficult to repeat their Stanley Cup-winning ways with a new team, so it is with business executives. They often have a very difficult time fitting into a new organization, finding acceptance in a new business culture, or creating the same level of success that they had attained for their previous employer. Their team members are different, and the business systems, relationships, and company culture are all different. In short, the context that helped them create their results has changed. They may not have known what made them successful in the first place! And even if they do know what worked at Company One, there is simply no guarantee that the same sort of solution will be applicable in Company Two.

Here's another striking example of this phenomenon. In 2004, the *Harvard Business Review* (*HBR*) published a study of 1,052 "star" stock analysts who worked for seventy-eight different investment banks in the United States between 1988 and 1996. The *HBR* article makes this sobering point: "Top performers resemble comets more than stars: once they're lured to another firm, their performance plummets by as much as 20 percent—permanently." The study found that only 30 percent of a star's performance can be traced to his or her individual skill or knowledge. The remaining 70 percent comes from the star's context, including specific attributes of his or her original company such as reputation, technology, leadership, training, and team chemistry. When new recruits left that context behind, they often couldn't recreate their former star power. Forty-six percent of transplanted analysts performed poorly in their first year at a new company. On average, performance dropped by 20 percent, and even five years later, it had not returned to previous levels. Furthermore, these new recruits were often so unable to adapt that 36 percent of them left their new bank within thirty-six months, and another 29 percent quit in the following twenty-four months, with a total of 65 percent leaving within five years.

Perhaps the most worrisome trend this article points out is that hiring talent from the outside often has a lasting adverse effect on the organization itself. Current employees are demoralized by the search for outside talent, and often they are passed over for resources allocated for the new stars. These interpersonal conflicts can throw a team off kilter for years.[7]

The Costs of Hiring

As if the risks involved in hiring outside talent weren't enough, the other major problem with recruiting is that you're going to have to spend a lot of money on it. You typically have to pay a high premium to attract a successful executive from a comfortable, winning niche. The kind of money you have to pay an outside hire can throw a salary structure out of whack, creating resentment among the people currently on your team who have worked so hard to build your organization to where it is right now. And, as I pointed out, you're taking a gamble that you won't get a good return on the salary investment. It may just be that the new executive will lack the energy and drive to duplicate prior success. You can't always "get the band back together." Or to change metaphors, Google at fifty was a steal. But what about Google at 500? A wise investment? Or is the upward potential still there?

Put all these factors together and, in most cases, you end up with a very strong case *against* buying talent. I'm not saying that hiring external talent is doomed to failure, no matter what. There are plenty of counter examples, and you may be one of them! But the reality is that for businesses, just as for sports teams, buying talent can often be an expensive exercise in frustration and can actually leave an organization worse off than before it made the move.

When greater focus is given to growing talent internally, these challenges are sidestepped. In addition, you gain the benefit of a predictable pipeline. You know what you have in terms of talent and, with the tools discussed later in this book, you'll also know where your talent stands vis-à-vis your organization and what their

7. Groysberg et al., "The Risky Business of Hiring Stars," Harvard Business Review (2004).

intentions are long term. Better yet, you can shape your ELs, providing the opportunities for them to learn the skill sets you'll need down the road. Essentially, you're able to create a pipeline of future leaders instead of taking a gamble on finding them externally, and rolling the dice again on the question of whether or not they'll integrate and generate the value you deserve.

The most important benefit of growing your talent is that it provides you with greater insulation against that demographic tsunami we know is coming. Your current employees understand your organization's culture. Presumably, they were originally attracted to it for a reason, and they continue to fit in with it now. They know the industry; they know your business, and they can hit the ground running when you call upon them to step into new roles. If that's the case, then your best strategy often isn't buying talent, it's growing talent.

Does this mean you should never hire outside talent? Of course not. Clearly there are times when hiring externally is a better course of action. Sometimes you simply don't have the skill set internally and you can't wait to develop it. Also, as a company you can only teach what you know and sometimes you just need to expand your current knowledge base. Obtaining people who possess certain knowledge or expertise currently possessed by your competition, for example, can be very helpful. Hiring outside talent can secure this information or expertise far more quickly than accumulating such knowledge or experience organically. Also, every now and then, things need to be shaken up by bringing in some fresh blood. But the primary emphasis in terms of long-term talent development needs to be on growing it rather than buying it, because buying it is often an expensive and unpredictable proposition that may come with a whole host of unintended consequences.

6

Separating the Wheat from the Chaff: Identifying the Right ELs for Your Enterprise

Stop and Listen to the Music

The Washington Post recently reported on a story that reveals an uncanny truth about human nature—and that might help you put the question of identifying your Emerging Leaders into perspective.

On a bitter January morning during rush hour, a man set up a music stand outside a bustling Washington, D.C. metro station and began to play the violin. He played six Bach pieces over a period of about forty-five minutes. It was later estimated that thousands of commuters passed him on their way in and out of the station.

The man played alone and unnoticed for three minutes before a middle-aged gentleman in a business suit paused to listen. He slowed his pace slightly as he passed, watching the violinist with curiosity. But the expression on his face quickly changed from interest to the familiar, grim purposefulness of the daily grind, and he continued on his way after only a few seconds.

The violinist received his first tip a minute later. A woman—also in business attire—tossed a dollar into his open case, but continued walking without even the briefest pause. The next admirer took more time. He leaned against a nearby building for several minutes to listen. Then a glance at his watch seemed to awaken him to the realities of his day, and he disappeared into the crowd of workers.

Finally, a three-year-old boy passed, his mother hurriedly tugging him along by the arm. He stopped in his tracks when he heard the music and stared at the violinist, mouth agape. But his mother pulled him after her, and all he could do was crane his neck to continue watching the violinist as they continued down the street.

The violinist played for forty-five minutes, and in all that time, only six people stopped to listen for more than a few moments. Roughly twenty dropped money in his case, without slowing their normal pace. When he finished playing and the sounds of traffic and harried businesspeople again took over the street corner, there was no applause, no recognition for the performance. The violinist collected $32.

He was Joshua Bell, one of the world's most renowned classical musicians. He was playing some of the most intricate and acclaimed compositions ever written, and performing them on a violin worth $3.5 million. Two days before his performance at the metro, Bell played a sold-out concert in Boston, where the seats went for an average of $100.

The *Post* organized Bell's performance as a social experiment about people's perceptions, tastes, and priorities. They wanted to explore what happens to our perception of beauty when it appears in a commonplace environment at an inappropriate hour. Can we notice it at all? Do we stop to appreciate it? Do we recognize talent in an unexpected context?

Reading this story, the inevitable question arises: If we do not have a moment to stop and listen to one of the best musicians in the world playing some of the best music ever written . . . what else are we missing? My hope for this chapter is to help you lift the veil, at least in your professional life, and to begin to find ways to take note of the talent that might be just under your nose. I will provide you with a general profile of what the emerging talent in your "rush-hour" business world looks like, so that you can separate the wheat from the chaff and start getting more from the hard work you—and your ELs—are already putting in.

Leave Trailing Indicators Behind

The challenge with regard to identifying ELs is that business leaders have traditionally focused solely on retention and engagement. In other words, all that matters is keeping people, and keeping them focused. These are incredibly important things, but the problem is that if these are the indicators by which you are measuring success, they only tell part of the story. They are "trailing indicators"—they tell you how well things have gone in the past. They don't speak to the issue of which people are likely to make the biggest difference in the future. Retention and engagement, as trailing indicators, are kind of like standing at the stern of a ship, looking backwards, studying the wake of a boat, and trying to steer around all the rocks off the ship's prow . . . while facing backwards. Not a recipe for success. Retention and engagement also can be deceptive, because the organization might just be retaining and engaging the wrong people!

So how can you know who the right people are?

In a word, it all comes down to fit. The question is not just how well they did in previous roles, because that only gives you part of the answer. The question is how will they do while in their next role. What skill set does the next role demand? Will they be able to grow into new responsibilities, and motivate others? So the questions to ask are really all about fit. Does the individual's leadership style and skill set fit with the organization and where it wants to go? And, in a short-term sense, does the individual fit with his or her manager? Is there compatibility?

Whatever you focus on, whatever you pay attention to most, is what you'll get back the most. And that's not always a good thing. For example, if a company suffered from high turnover and wanted to fix this problem, it might put in metrics to reward managers with high retention rates of staff members. The problem again is that maybe we're retaining the wrong people. How the organization measures performance really makes a difference. It's that old story: Be careful what you wish for. It shouldn't be about how many people you are retaining. It should be about the question of whether you are retaining people who fit well with your company's mission and where it wants to go in the *future.*

In his best-selling book, *Good to Great,* business author Jim Collins uses the expression "on the bus" to describe the ideal situation in terms of executive recruitment and retention. You want to have the right people in the right seats on the bus, and then you can get somewhere. Typically, people bring me into a company when the seats on the bus are already filled. My job isn't so much putting people in the right seat on the bus. My job is making sure that the bus will have a sufficient pool of competent drivers in the future! I help guide companies to give their ELs the training and experience so that when it comes time for them to drive the bus—whether it's a minibus in the form of a department or division of the company, or whether they need to take over the driver's seat of the whole organization—they'll be ready. Will they be able to drive just one bus or will they be able to drive a fleet of buses? Companies must concern themselves not only with "right person in the right seat on the bus" but the question of creating bus drivers for the future. That's the only way you ensure that the bus will head in the right direction long after the current occupants have moved on, switched seats, or gotten off the road altogether.

So how do you choose the next generation of bus drivers? The first step is to *identify* your Emerging Leader profile. What's the typical profile of an EL in your organization? What skills and traits and culture does your company need to get you where you want to go? The second phase is *selecting*—both internally and, if necessary, externally—the candidates who best fit, or could fit, the profile you've created. We'll talk about these two phases in general in this chapter, and in chapter 7, I'll give you some actionable tools for selection.

Part I: Identification—Create Your Emerging Leader Profile

Identifying the ELs you want and need begins with understanding the culture of your company. What's your company all about? Where is it going? Some organizations, such as Google, are very creative and innovative. Others, especially many in the financial services industry, cannot be as creative in the same way, by virtue of the strict regulations that affect the nature of products they can offer. This means that no EL is going to be right for all companies, or for the cultures of all industries. Most Senior Leaders have a clearer idea about the value proposition of their products and services, and about what their target market constitutes, than about the value proposition for prospective and existing employees. In other words, companies know more about whom they're selling to than whom they want to attract and retain as employees.

As a result, one of the current popular topics in the area of organizational development is the idea of employee branding. What is your brand proposition as an employer? If an EL came to your organization, would they find it a creative, entrepreneurial place to work, or one that values conservative approaches and long-term strategic business acumen? Different cultures will fit differently with different ELs. That's the kind of conversation now going on in the marketplace: how do you, as an organization, want to position yourselves to prospective and current employees?

In order to tackle that critically important question, it's necessary to step back and ask these questions: Who is important for this organization's future? What does the organization need from its people in order to move forward and be competitive in the future? And what type of culture do we have in place right now, or would we like to have in place, in order to be competitive in the future? This context should be considered when determining what kind of ELs you want to attract, retain, and grow. Management guru Peter Drucker said that the fundamental question a business must ask is this: "What kind of business are we in?" Until a company can answer that with a reasonable degree of accuracy, it's all but impossible to determine which ELs are appropriate to take the company to the next level.

Companies that understand where they are going as an entity in the marketplace make much more meaningful and useful decisions about the identification, selection, and development of Emerging Leaders. The more clarity companies have about how they want to develop and grow, about what systems within the organization make the most sense, about what the culture of the organization is, and *fundamentally about the capabilities they'll need to get there*, the more fruitful their identification and selection practices will become.

As an example, I was recently approached by a medium-sized company that makes equipment used in the aircraft industry. They have been very successful in the past, but the VP of HR confided in me that management was still terribly "old-school" and operates out of a very old command-and-control management style. In order for them to be competitive in the long run, they will need to become extremely innovative with their products and services right now. But current management simply doesn't support innovative thinking and approaches. So before they can tackle the question of whom to select, train, and promote, in a global way, they have to focus on the threshold issues of "Who do we want to be in the marketplace going forward?" and "What type of employees and ELs do we need to get us there?"

Like many companies, once it defines its employee culture this company will be able to determine with more clarity just who the right people are to keep on the bus . . . and to train as future bus drivers. This comes back to the earlier point we discussed about importing talent. If you hire someone from outside the company who does not fit into the culture, or who may be from a totally different culture, in the long term, it is going to be an uphill struggle both for that individual and for the company. Think John Scully and Apple.

The same is true with selecting and identifying talent internally. If we pick people who do not work well with the culture the company either has or wishes to have, then it will be an uphill struggle for all concerned. My role in all this is not so much to help a company create a culture identity but instead to point out to companies the importance of understanding what their culture is. At that point, we can then talk about retaining and promoting those individuals who fit well with the culture of the company. Because, as I said earlier, fit is the single most important criterion.

Is the company very sales-oriented? Is the company more interested in research and development? How are decisions made—is the structure very "top down," where there is a directive and then everybody follows it? Or is it more collaborative, where management presents an initiative and defines an expected result, and then a whole bunch of people work together on that initiative in a collaborative way? Is it a fun, casual environment, or is it really intense and competitive? Or both? How would you describe to someone else the experience of working in this organization?

Ironically, an organization can begin this process of thinking about which ELs to promote and quickly find itself with a much larger question: Where are we trying to go as an organization? So the challenge of identifying the right ELs can turn into an opportunity for rethinking and shifting the entire culture of the organization.

Organizations often shy away from the entire question of which ELs to focus on because they are too time-strapped or uninterested to think about the future in a meaningful way from a leadership perspective. I like to think of choosing the right ELs in terms of picking the right furniture for one's home. You really have two choices. You can just go out and buy a bunch of stuff that will be functional but perhaps mismatched—a dining table in a style that clashes with the dining room chairs, which doesn't match the living room furniture, which doesn't match the kitchen furniture. Or you can take time and say, "What kind of home do I want to have?" And then you can go out and get one nice piece at a time in keeping with that overall view of how you want your home to look. So it is in organizations—they can either fill spaces with warm bodies, or they can think through a comprehensive vision of where they want to be in the future and then attract, retain, and develop the right kind of people to get them there.

Thinking about the future in this way is always at odds with putting out the fires occurring right now. At the end of the American Civil War, when Atlanta was burning, there wasn't much call for urban planners! But the reality is that, in business,

Atlanta is *always* burning. There is always a crisis to be managed, a fire to be put out, a major project off the rails, a big deal that just won't close. It's natural for senior management to direct its time, attention, and focus to crisis management. But as we know, crisis management and business management are not the same things. At some point, an organization must be willing to commit to the idea of spending critical resources—time, money, energy, and focus—on creating the next generation of ELs. Otherwise, the company will not have a next generation at all. Worse still—your competition will have yours.

A Typical Emerging Leader Profile

To drill down from the organization level to the individual level and identify what a typical Emerging Leader might look like, let's refer back to the definition of an Emerging Leader:

Emerging Leader: *Someone whose ability to make change—that they believe in—is developing, coming into existence, and coming forth into view or notice.*

From a demographic perspective, ELs are often in the range of 30 to 45 years old, although they truly can be any age. They have begun to establish a track record in business, but they don't necessarily have the sense of confidence that many years of experience can bring. The career experimentation and exploration days of their twenties are behind them. It's natural for most thirty-year-olds to have greater clarity about what they want to do professionally, and about what's important to them. Moreover, they might be facing the increased personal responsibilities of starting a family, which demands much greater commitment and focus professionally, or have become heavily involved with other outside interests. Most importantly, they are thirsty for the right challenges that will help them grow and establish themselves.

This is a unique period of a leader's evolution, in which greater clarity and focus is formed. It often is accompanied by a dramatically increased sense of personal responsibility (and often stability), all without habits and approaches that have been ingrained for decades. It's fertile ground, and a formative time.

But not every thirty-something manager is an Emerging Leader. Remember, the key distinguishing factor is the EL's *willingness to make change they believe in.* The profile below highlights some other intangible qualities that mark these individuals.

Typical Profile of an Emerging Leader

Age range: 30–45*

Attitudes: A "go-getter," does what it takes, willing to learn and initiate change that they believe in; I am a Me, Inc.

Attributes: Energetic, committed

Ambitions: To have an interesting, challenging career that can work with personal priorities

Personal priorities: Juggling professional ambitions with a young family and/or active personal life

Professional results: Sometimes shorter but promising track record of success

Organization views him/her as: "High-potential" or an "up-and-comer"

*Again, as outlined in the opening section of the book, this is not a hard and fast time frame. Typically, we do certain types of things at certain ages—but there are always exceptions. This is also a typical time frame when an individual has greater capacity to contribute to the organization, and the impact of the EL's efforts is therefore easier to see.

Part 2: Selection—Who Fits Your Emerging Leader Profile?

Once you've identified your EL profile, we can begin to focus on the central question of this part of the book: Which ones do you keep, and why? The matrix below provides a simple, yet effective place to begin that inquiry. The intention is to, in a straightforward way, categorize who are the value producers (ELs) in your organization and why.

The Value Producer Matrix: The Four Quadrants

RESULTS / BEHAVIOUR	UNCONSTRUCTIVE	CONSTRUCTIVE
HIGH	**Q1 DOMINANT PRODUCER** **Possible fit** **RESULTS ORIENTATION:** · highly proactive · track record of results · exceeds/meets targets · problem solver **BEHAVIOURS:** · not open to new/others' ideas · dominates vs. collaborates · poor listener · task-only focus · can blame situation on others	**Q2 LONG-TERM PRODUCER** **Great fit** **RESULTS ORIENTATION:** · highly proactive · track record of results · exceeds/meets targets · problem solver **BEHAVIOURS:** · continual learner · collaborates/shares ideas · active listener · task *and* people focus · takes accountability
LOW	**Q3 LOW PRODUCER** **Poor fit** **RESULTS ORIENTATION:** · more reactive/less proactive · little/no track record of results · just meets or misses targets · waits for direction **BEHAVIOURS:** · not open to new/others' ideas · dominates vs. collaborates · poor listener · task-only focus · blames circumstances or others	**Q4 EMERGING PRODUCER** **Excellent fit** **RESULTS ORIENTATION:** · more reactive/less proactive · shorter track record of results · inconsistently hits targets · may wait for direction **BEHAVIOURS:** · continual learner · collaborates/shares ideas · active listener · task and people focus · takes accountability

Here the Y axis is Results—are they producing high results or low results?—and the X axis represents Behaviour—is the behaviour that they use to produce results constructive or unconstructive? When you begin to plot your ELs against this matrix, you begin to consider the behaviours that you really want in the organization. This is the link between the cultural questions of "Where are we going strategically?" and "What are the behaviours that will get us where we want to go?"

Quadrant 1: The Dominant Producer. Quadrant 1 people are results-orientated, highly proactive, have a track record of results, are meeting or exceeding targets, and are problem-solvers. They're out there just creating results. On paper, they look as though they are producing, that they are stars or at least very high-calibre individuals. And yet, there's often a distinction between the way people look on paper and what's going on in real life. That's why we want to consider behaviour as something as important as results.

Unconstructive behaviour could include individuals who are not open to other people's ideas or to new ideas in general. They aren't learners. They'll tend to do things the same way or their way. They can dominate instead of collaborate. They can be prima donnas. I believe that anyone can be trained out of bad behaviours, as long as they are willing. As long as there is a true desire to learn or change, anything is possible.

Often, employers are willing to overlook bad behaviour because of the good results the person generates. Yes, dominant producers can generate great results, but they also can kill off the team. Because these individuals are often so task-only focused, they often don't think about the impact on the people around them as they drive for results. These individuals are more about short-term success instead of building relationships that are key for long-term success. They don't think about the cost to you or your organization that their behaviour incurs. They may also tend to brush off accountability for their behaviour. These individuals tend to be less self-aware. Sometimes they're conscious of the fact that their behaviour is inappropriate in an organization, and sometimes they are unconscious of that fact. Again, they can be trained out of those behaviours, as long as you're willing to take the time to work with them and as long as they are willing to try things a different way.

In the right circumstances these individuals are sometimes the ones who can grow the most through the kind of training I provide. Perhaps they have been succeeding for a while, and suddenly they've been shot down. They might have made a major mistake, or they got some kind of wake-up call telling them that what they are doing is no longer working. In that case, it might be a very ripe time for me to start working with that individual.

I recall working with one person in particular in this Quadrant who had produced remarkable results but who had caused such internal unrest that an ombudsman was called in and an external report was generated. This became a real opportunity for this leader to take a look at what he was doing, because the evidence clearly pointed toward him as the cause of the problems. He was able to shift his attitudes and behaviours, and as a result, he was able to do great things for the company and indeed his career. Investing in Quadrant 1 ELs tends to be highly individual, more than it is with individuals in any other Quadrant. Success in developing these ELs is entirely contingent on their attitude, and their willingness to change, accept new ideas, and honestly reflect on any negative impact their behaviours have had on the organization.

Quadrant 2: The Long-Term Producer. In Quadrant 2 we find the people who already have the great track record to go along with the great results. They have already figured out the behaviours that are necessary to succeed, and they already have an extensive track record that demonstrates success. These are the stars in any organization. It doesn't take a genius to recognize their value, now and in the future, to an organization. If you've got them, be grateful, and take good care of them! The people in Quadrant 2 are leaders who have already emerged, so to speak.

They can also be great fits for leadership development, depending on where they are. They're results-oriented, proactive, and have a track record of results. They're very similar to the dominant producers in Quadrant 1 as far as their results orientation goes. They meet targets and they're problem-solvers.

At the same time, long-term producers are continual learners and team players, and this is what separates them from the individuals in Quadrant 1. They also want to learn about what's going on around them, about themselves, about their teams, about their markets, about how the organization as a whole is going. They're always looking to learn, and they are very receptive to feedback or ideas. As a result, they tend to be much more collaborative. They share ideas instead of hoarding information. For them, it's not just about reaching the result—it's also about asking, "How do we get there? And at what cost?" These are the people who believe that you measure success not only by what you achieve but by what you had to give up in order to get it. They're the ones who ask whether they had to burn a bunch of bridges in order to get a particular short-term result. They want to know whether they had to burn out their employees in order to get a project out on time, instead of renegotiating a deadline. That's why I say they are both task-focused and people-focused. Individuals in Quadrant 2 know that the people side is part of the long-term picture.

In the 1970s and '80s, in the command-and-control approach to business, life was more about Quadrant 1 workers, individuals who were more predominantly results-orientated and created more of the "My way or the highway" kind of folks. Their approach defined business after World War II and created the hierarchical structures of business that prevailed up to the end of the twentieth century. Under this model, there was less concern about the human element of the equation. Of course, Quadrant 2 managers existed, but the prevailing business culture primarily rewarded results only, and not how the results were achieved.

Today, society is changing, for the reasons we outlined in the initial chapters of this book. ELs simply won't tolerate Quadrant 1 behaviours for long, and with the employment opportunities out there, they don't have to. The people who are in favour are the ones who have the ability to actively listen, who are both task- and people-focused, and who are concerned not just about the results, but also about how they're getting there. They are accountable—not just for results, but also for how the results are produced. Clearly, Quadrant 2 workers are great people to hang onto. They will add enormous value to any organization, and they will do it in a way that's aligned with what ELs expect and are beginning to demand.

Quadrant 3: The Low Producers. These are the people who are a poor fit for any organization, let alone any kind of leadership development initiative. They don't have a results orientation, and they tend to be more reactive and less proactive. They have little or no track record of results. They just meet targets, or they consistently miss targets. They're the ones who are waiting for direction.

As far as behaviours, the low producers are not open to new ideas. Their attitude is, "This is the way it's been done, and this is the way it'll always be done." Clearly, these are not people you want to hang onto. Individuals who are poor listeners and tend to blame circumstances or other people for their problems are exactly the people who have no future in your organization. Let them go to your competitors! As Dr. Nick Bontis, the Director of the Institute for Intellectual Capital Research, says, "In today's world, unless you're willing to renew, relearn, retool, re-certify, and re-professionalize, then you had better be prepared to retire!"

Emerging Leaders understand this proposition intuitively. They know that if they aren't prepared to reinvent themselves and continually learn and stay marketable, they'll be toast. That takes us back to the Me, Inc. discussion. Ironically, if someone isn't a Me, Inc.—intent on growth and development, always with one eye on the next opportunity to add value (internally or externally)—they're dramatically less likely to lead change. The people who will make the biggest difference for you are the ones who are constantly looking to add value to the company and to the customers.

Quadrant 4: The Emerging Producer (also known as the Emerging Leader). It's the people in Quadrant 4 on whom this book focuses: the ones whose potential to add value is evidenced by their behaviours and not necessarily by their track records, yet. These are the up-and-coming producers, and they are an excellent fit for most leadership development initiatives. Often, they haven't been in the business world quite as long as their peers in Quadrants 1 and 2, so they may have a shorter track record of results. They may be hitting targets inconsistently, and they may wait for direction in certain situations. But they can be trained to move from reactivity to pro-activity, so their track records should not be a deal-killer when you're considering them for leadership opportunities.

Emerging Leaders demonstrate the right behaviours much of the time, and have produced some great results, although perhaps on a smaller scale or inconsistently. One of the most critically important behaviours that an EL can demonstrate is that of being a continual learner. This comes up again and again in discussions with senior leaders: the ability to learn and be open to new ideas, to collaborate, to share ideas (and credit) with others, to be an active listener, and to have a task-and-people focus. It's not just about the job, but how the job is done.

An individual like this might have very strong behaviours in these areas but might not necessarily have produced great results yet. Or perhaps they have not yet produced results in a consistent fashion, either because they are inexperienced or because they are still trying to figure things out. A young executive can be overwhelmed by all of the tasks that he or she must face. Much like the people who missed Joshua Bell playing violin at the subway station, it can be all too easy to overlook the individual with the right skills and behaviours in favour of the person who has weaker skills but a stronger track record. Yet individuals who possess these highly important behaviours are often extremely good fits for leadership development investments, because the internal makeup of a leader is there—even if the long-term track record is not. So it's essential for managers to be able to look beyond the immediate bottom line and instead look at the *behaviours and character* of an Emerging Leader, to determine whether that individual has what it takes to continue to grow and succeed.

So, let's talk about the behaviour of Quadrant 4 types. We talked in an earlier chapter about the lack of confidence of the EL, which is a function of the shorter track record of results. In general, their behaviours are highly constructive, and the more they succeed, and the more opportunities they are given to succeed, the more their confidence will grow. They share with Quadrant 2 the highly constructive behaviours demanded by the next generation of employees: they are continual learners, they collaborate, they share ideas, and they're active listeners. They're both task- and people-focused, and they take an above average level of accountability for what they do. Emerging Leaders have the behaviours of

Quadrant 2 people, but they don't yet have the track record. It will come. Now that they're starting to get serious about their careers, they're rolling up their sleeves a bit more and perhaps getting a bit more focused. The track record will build over time. These are your Emerging Leaders.

To put it all together, we want to move people in Quadrant 4 up to Quadrant 2. We want to move Quadrant 1 folks over to Quadrant 2, and we want to move Quadrant 2 producers further up. And Quadrant 3? It's time to move them out.

Overlooked Success Factors: Attitude, Outlook, and Personality

Typically, when SLs are seeking to select the ELs to take them into the future, they look at the technical side of knowledge, education, and skills—all of which are valid. But what you really need to heavily consider are these intangibles: the attitude, values, and personality of the individual, and whether they fit with your culture or team. In today's rapidly changing world, skills and formal education are outdated in record time and technical competence is increasingly "off-shored." What is becoming far more important is the individual's capability to embrace development, to learn and respond to a changing environment and to work with and through people.

This pressure to adapt and work more effectively with people is compounded by the very nature of becoming a leader and now being responsible for others. As The Value Producer Matrix illustrates, the demands on their human competence and strategic skill set increase while the dependence on their technical competence diminishes. My point here is to advise you to rely less on past "technical" competencies and success and instead focus on what drives an individual's behaviours (and success) in the longer-term: their personality, attitudes, and outlook.

The Value Producer Matrix—Actions

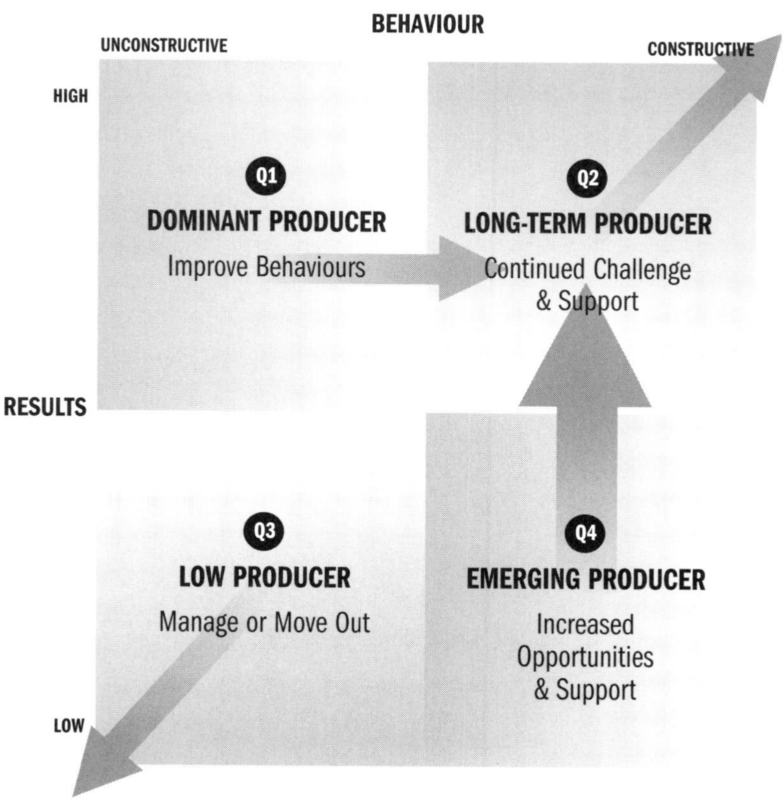

Quadrant 1: High results but unconstructive behaviour
Quadrant 2: Constructive behaviour and high results
Quadrant 3: Poor behaviour, poor results
Quadrant 4: The results aren't consistently there yet, but their behaviour is constructive

Below is a list of the questions that can help you decide if a candidate is likely to be a natural fit for you. Leadership development initiatives with individuals who share most of these traits will pay big dividends. These attitudes and outlooks foster the soft side, the behaviour axis of the Value-Producer Matrix.

Competencies for Success in Career Stages

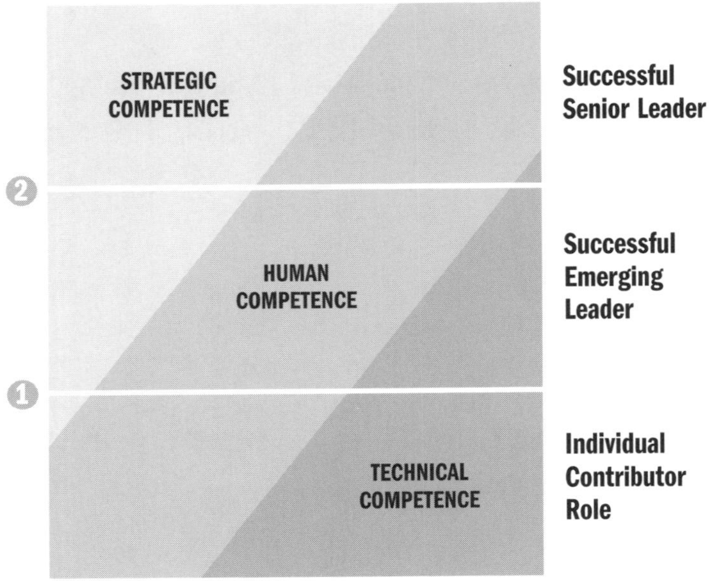

1 and 2: Key Career Transition Points that Require New and/or Different Competencies

When you consider a candidate for leadership development, ask yourself: Is this person . . .

Genuine and open?
Committed to success?
Willing to take ownership?
Eager to contribute?
Passionate about excellence?
Prepared to make change and take appropriate risk?

Aware of the importance of supportive relationships?
Respectful of themselves and others?
Able to laugh at themselves?

Free Bonus Resource–The Best Fit Index

In addition to asking the questions above, you might also find it useful to use our quick selection tool on the Footprint Leadership Web site. **In a few short minutes you'll be able to gauge the likelihood that investing in your leadership development candidate(s) will generate the ROI your company deserves. Find out how to access it for free on the back page of this book.**

Here's what I mean by each of the above qualities. Prize ELs have an openness to new ideas and the willingness to acknowledge their own shortcomings, at least in private conversation. It's a commitment to success, which speaks to their results orientation. They possess the go-getter's approach, the commitment to making things happen, and they take responsibility for making it so. They have a strong desire to contribute to something that's bigger than they are. It's the passion for excellence—they have no interest in being average or in producing average results. It's the willingness to take appropriate risk, because they understand that risk is the key to playing a bigger game and making change.

They don't always take the risk—that's because they're still emerging, right? But they are the ones who are taking more risks than the Quadrant 3s, the low producers who don't put up their hand and who don't take any chances. And this means that you, as the senior leader, must be willing to give them enough rope to fail at different things. As Wayne Gretzky (a childhood hockey hero of mine) said, "You miss one hundred percent of the shots you don't take." These people are out there taking shots, and not all of them will find the back of the net. But any hockey player knows that you learn to shoot by practicing! And if you have enough shots on goal, eventually something is going to get by the goalkeeper. The people who are out there taking shots are the ones you want to keep.

Finally, the last trait you want to look for in an Emerging Leader is a good sense of humour. They don't have to be comedians or raconteurs, but they should have the ability to look at the lighter side of life. This indicates a sense of maturity and an understanding that we're not as important as we often make ourselves out to be. We have to be able to laugh at ourselves, or as the expression goes, we're missing out on the biggest joke of all. Nobody's perfect. We screw up all the time, and you know what? It's all going to work out in the long run. People who have a great sense of humor about themselves and the world around them tend to make better, happier, stronger, and more grounded leaders. And those are the Emerging Leaders you want to keep.

7

Who Makes the Final Cut? Selecting Your Emerging Leaders

Once you have a sense of your company culture and a clearer idea of the characteristics inherent in a successful Emerging Leader, you're better equipped to move on to the actual process of selection. How do you choose the ELs in your organization? Who will be the best fit, so that together, you can create the most value—and heck, have the most fun? In this chapter, I'll give you some Tools for Selection that will allow you to proactively select your ELs and increase the odds of the best fit. But first, I'd like to warn against a particular approach many organizations employ—the "self-selection" approach.

Avoid the Pitfalls of "Self-Selection"

My proactive philosophy contrasts many traditional approaches, which may prefer that ELs "self-select." Instead of the SLs saying, "Let's choose the people we think are good fits for this organization and approach them," they wait for ELs to "demonstrate their leadership and readiness to do so." They wait for them to assertively ask for more work and more responsibilities. While the rationale of this approach may have worked in past decades, when talent was plenty and loyalty strong, times have clearly changed. Failing to recognize the potential of your ELs and, instead, waiting for them to put up their hands and say, "Give me more," can lead to losing your best people. Some of your best ELs may not be the traditional, aggressive, and extroverted Type-A executives. They might be asking for opportunities less aggressively—and as a result, you might not even hear them asking.

In addition, there are the ELs who are absolutely ideal candidates as future leaders of your organization, but who aren't actively courting additional responsibility for fear of getting too much dumped on their plate. They're simply not prepared to dedicate more time *at this time*. They may be interested, eager, and truly committed to the organization, but their non-work priorities keep them from translating that commitment into the kind of mega-hours that SLs might have put in at the same point in their career, twenty or thirty years ago when expectations were different. Remember, typical ELs are highly engaged in other areas of life. When dedication to family or balancing work with other facets of one's life is dictating the behaviour of your ELs, it can be hard to tell which ELs really want to take on more and move up.

ELs in their thirties and forties—typically the child-raising years—can appear disinterested. Sometimes they aren't volunteering for extra responsibility, and they may even request to work *less*, as we discussed in previous chapters. It's crucial to understand that for these ELs, lack of motivation or ambition is not the problem. In fact, many of them would be eager to create a win-win situation that allows them both to advance and to hold on to their flexibility. However, relying on them to self-select at this stage will often yield a disappointing number of candidates for your company. Also, if the organization chooses the "wait and see" approach, the EL may assume he or she is not on the "up-and-comer" list. Would you rather the nod of acknowledgment of both their potential and their situation come from you or from one of the countless recruiters knocking on their door? In a world of diminished supply of qualified talent, it's a no-brainer.

Proactive Tools for Selection

Given that I don't advocate the "wait for them" approach, how do I suggest that you make informed choices when you select the employees on whom you will focus greater energy in developing and retaining?

Unfortunately, there's no silver bullet here. Everything I provide in terms of my consulting, as well as the information and tools like the Value Producer Matrix in this book, are guideposts, but there is no silver bullet for making the right choice. Selection is both an art and a science. There's a human element—instinct or intuition. Then there's an aspect of hardcore facts related to measurable performance. So the question really becomes this: What tools can you use—either on the soft side, like intuition or instinct, or hard data—to help you make the best choice possible?

Before you can begin, you have to be aware of two Key Cautionary Points:

1. Stay focused on long-term performance.
2. Be aware of your own biases.

Let's take a closer look at each of these Key Cautionary Points.

1. Long-term performance.

This may sound counterintuitive, given that emerging leaders tend not to have long track records of success. The point here is that, when selecting an EL in which to invest, you must focus on the longest-term performance you can and not the recent past. An individual might have been doing quite well for a period of time, but might have bombed on his or her last project. That shouldn't take that EL out of the running. Conversely, they might have bombed on their first project and may have been doing pretty well since. It's essential to examine long-term performance rather than just take a short-term view, because everyone is going to make mistakes at some point in his or her career. Don't get sidetracked by one glitzy success or one abysmal failure.

The alternative is to look for people who have near-perfect or blunder-free records. But more often than not, such records point to individuals who've never been innovative or really taken a leadership risk. And given that today's business world demands leaders who can make, manage, and mold change, clearly you want to keep in your organization the people who are out there taking appropriate chances, who are swinging out, and who are doing things that have not been done before. And when that happens, when people have that kind of freedom, there will be failure. There will be mistakes. Just like the stock market, we always want to look at the long-term trend, or at least to make that view as long term as possible.

Consider the entire career, and not just the most recent success or failure. It's a little like judging in some sporting events where the highest and lowest scores are pulled out of the mix and the balance of scores form the basis for scoring. This is also true for those who don't have a long track record with your organization or who are simply younger employees, perhaps in their twenties. Later in this chapter, we'll talk about work-life history interviews, a tool to help you examine the long-term with these employees.

2. Be aware of your own biases.

It's essential to take into consideration the biases we all have in terms of selecting people. There are five big ones that you should be aware of.

1. The Saint Effect. As the expression goes, beauty is in the eye of the beholder. And what makes an EL "attractive" in the eyes of an SL might be that he has a specific trait or experience or ability, one thing that the individual does astonishingly well that towers over the rest of his skill set. But in reality, as a complete package, the EL may not be all that great. It's easy to get blinded by that one dazzling ability or trait, so much so that you're seeing that employee from a limited perspective instead of seeing them in the context of *all* their strengths and weaknesses.

2. What have you done for me lately? It's not commonly known that it's often the *last* thing you've read or seen about a subject that most influences your current opinion about that same subject. The same is true in the case of assessing performance of your Emerging Leaders. What have you done for me lately? If you bombed recently, or something didn't go well, a bias against that person may offset excellent results that the person achieved in the past. But just because you haven't seen a big result lately, that doesn't mean the potential isn't still there. Conversely, a recent victory can cloud a pattern of unconstructive behaviour that hasn't been corrected.

3. The Just-Like-Me Bias. Another form of bias comes about simply in terms of personal comfort. I've talked about this many times with my Senior Leaders, and it all comes down to a personal bias, a subjective feeling about an EL that cannot always be put into words. It sounds something like this: "I just do not like that person. For whatever reason, he rubbed me the wrong way in a meeting or on a sales call or [fill in the blank]." Or its converse: "I always seem to get along with him; we just click." This sense of liking or disliking someone is frequently rooted in the bias against people who are not "like me."

Managers traditionally hire people who are just like themselves or as close to themselves as the market will provide. The subconscious thinking that dictates this choice goes something like this: "I'm very good at what I do, and if people are like me, then they'll be able to do the job well. Also, if they're just like me, I'll get along with them, they'll be fun to work with, and they'll make my life easier. They have similar ideas and a similar world view. Boy, they must be fantastic."

The problem here is that you can end up getting a whole bunch of people who are just like the SL, who will never challenge the status quo, and who will never take the organization to another level. Instead of looking at every candidate with fresh eyes, this kind of manager unconsciously screens out people who do not resemble his thinking, appearance, outside interests, world-view, socioeconomic level, and sometimes ethnic background or other traits. This approach might have been acceptable or even laudatory a generation or two ago. Today, though, in an environment that demands constant change and reinvention, this kind of bias is a recipe for disaster.

4. The Good Guy Factor. These people are nice, likeable, and produce "okay" results. They're "good people" who work hard. The Good Guy Factor may gloss over missing skill sets or poor behaviours. It's the same thing that can deter performance-improvement conversations. They're a "good guy," they do their best, but good intentions alone don't produce results.

5. The Fire-Fighting Bias. Another subtle problem that arises when it comes to the process of talent evaluation is the fact that some senior managers simply don't see the value in the talent management process itself. Sometimes they haven't been exposed to the articles in business journals about the phenomenon of baby boomers retiring, a talent war, and the shortage of younger workers. That's understandable, given their focus. Their overall reaction to a talent management exercise such as this is to shrug their shoulders and say, "I've got a business line to run, let HR handle it."

Many managers are more concerned with the immediate-term than the future of the company and its leadership. With the day-to-day pressures of running a business, this is an easy trap to fall into, and it leads to a bias against the entire process of identifying and engaging Emerging Leaders. The enlightened Senior Leader must recognize this bias in himself or in other SLs, and root it out if it is present. Indeed, identifying and growing Emerging Leaders can be a colossal waste of time unless senior management truly buys into the process.

If Senior Leaders tasked with the care and feeding of ELs get the sense that top management is simply paying lip service to the whole concept, but isn't really very committed to the idea of growing leaders, then the whole thing is an exercise in futility. Those at the highest levels of any organization must be committed to the recognition and development of the best ELs, because otherwise we are simply wasting time. This isn't so much a bias issue as it is a critical success factor, but I mention it here because it can represent the bias of individuals involved in the process as well as the bias of an entire organization against spending resources on the process of selecting and growing ELs.

The EL Selection Pyramid

Now that we have established the biases that an individual or an organization as a whole might have with regard to this whole business of selecting the right ELs for the future, and we've identified what kind of EL is best for us, the question becomes: "How do we select them?" What follows are a number of tools and approaches to answering that very question. You can organize these tools into what I call the "EL Selection Pyramid." Each of these tools helps you answer a specific question about your candidate: What? How? Or Who?

The EL Selection Pyramid

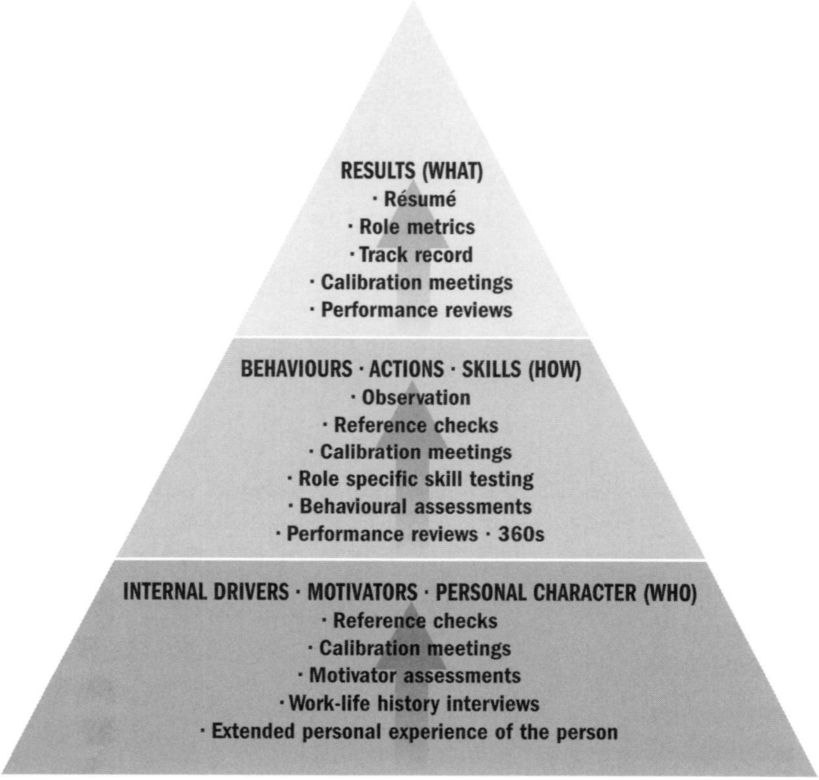

The peak of the pyramid is:

1. What? What are the *results* this candidate is capable of producing or has produced? We actually touched upon this question in the previous chapter, with the Value Producer Matrix. The answer to this question is traditionally found in performance management tools, specific job metrics, and technical skills tests. "What?" is only the tip of the iceberg—it's the most tangible measurement of what people can see. It is what ends up on a résumé, but it doesn't necessarily give you a sense of the source of the results.

The next layers of the pyramid are:

2. How? How are the results achieved? There are almost an infinite number of ways in which to produce a result and get a job done. What *behaviours* does your prospective EL demonstrate to produce their results?

3. Who? This question is about *internal drivers, motivation, and personal character.* It points to the character traits I outlined in the previous chapter. It is the "Who" of the individual (and pyramid) that drives the "How," which in turn drives and produces the results, the "What."

In what follows, I'll provide an overview of the common tools that are available to give you a holistic picture of the candidate. Indeed, the selection tools I'll introduce here focus mainly on the layers of the pyramid—the How and Who—and work to complement the traditional tools, such as résumés and typical performance reviews, which organizations traditionally rely on to point to the results apex of the pyramid—the What.

First are *assessments*. These are powerful and often under-utilized tools that can address both the "Who" and the "What" of the pyramid. As a company, it's your responsibility to decide what kind of person you're looking for. Once you've done that, you can begin to assess people to see how closely they match up with your needs, whether on an organizational level or a role level.

There are a host of personality assessments available to measure or predict people's behaviour and areas of interest. For example, some individuals are naturally interested in leading people. Some are more interested in learning new things. If you take a "learner" and place her in a position where she doesn't have an option to learn new things, she'll die on the vine, no matter how nice her boss is. So it's important to identify your ELs' natural drivers and whether they fit your needs.

One useful process for measuring fit is "job benchmarking." This is where you take people who have performed well in a role and benchmark their strengths as a guideline to show what you want to find in an EL slated to take that position. You could also take five different people who have succeeded in a role and compile a profile, and then match people to that profile. Arguably, this gets more challenging the higher up in the organization you go and the more sophisticated the role is. But it can provide valuable insight into particular roles where the expectations are relatively clear and consistent and there is a big enough sample size of current, past, and potential candidates to warrant the exercise.

Reference checks are a very basic tool, but they can be so important in determining "Who" and "How" that they bear mentioning. If you're recruiting someone new into your department, you want to know how they performed in the past. It's common sense—yet sometimes in the craziness of "we gotta fill this role fast" this rich evaluation opportunity gets overlooked in favour of résumés or performance reviews. It makes sense to speak with their manager (whether internal or external) about what worked and what didn't work in previous assignments. What are their strengths? What are their weaknesses? What were they *really* like to work with? What do we need to look out for? What potential do you think they have? Where do you see them going professionally? Even if you hire the individual anyway, why not benefit from the learning of the previous manager? Then you'll avoid making the same mistakes, and you'll leapfrog ahead.

Along the same lines, another important tool is the *performance review*. Most managers already do some form of a performance review, whether it's one-on-one or a 360-degree approach. We'll talk about this in more depth later in the book.

Another tool is the *calibration meeting*. Calibration meetings are excellent tools to use when assessing multiple existing staff. They also help address the challenges of rater bias we discussed above. One of the best ways to reduce or eliminate rater bias is to choose a number of different raters and then hold calibration meetings, where the selected SLs of the management team can debate the merits of individuals, instead of a single SL relying on his or her single opinion of a given EL. This can be used in conjunction with the Value Producer Matrix, so that as a group you vote on where each person fits in the matrix and, more importantly, why.

The *work-history interview* is perhaps the most powerful tool available to you when evaluating candidates. The most talent-savvy organizations rely heavily on this technique. Indeed, they would never make a selection decision without such a dialogue. At the end of the day, nothing can ever replace a probing interactive conversation where both parties are free to ask and answer questions.

The interview focuses on the work history of the EL, walking through his or her entire career, from the very beginning until today. When start and end dates are noted, this inquiry produces a career map that, in of itself, provides a unique and powerful insight into the EL's history of success and achievement.

The work-history interview goes well beyond a résumé. While this process will shed light on "what" they accomplished, and "how" they did it, its real value is to highlight the "who/why" side of the pyramid. It uncovers patterns of behaviour, which in turn point to the EL's character and, essentially, what he is all about—what drives him, his passions, ambitions, goals, concerns, fears, level of discipline, strengths, weaknesses, flexibility, biases, ability to achieve, and feelings about relationships. The interview can be done with the final candidates of a hiring process or with all internally identified and selected ELs.

The key to a successful interview is for you to make it as nonthreatening as possible. You can call it a getting acquainted session, where you sit down in a private setting, over a cup of coffee, and learn a little more about the person's background than the information that appears on the standard résumé.

I mentioned earlier the importance of bias. It's highly likely that the interviewer will have some form of opinion, whether positive or negative, about the individual before having this meeting, often based on the "just like me" bias. Rather than fishing for information that backs this opinion, I encourage the interviewer to challenge his hypothesis and not attempt to prove that his opinion is right. It doesn't serve the SL or the organization to hire people who just don't fit.

How do you begin this kind of conversation? My favourite approach is to have the SL simply ask, "Tell me about your first job." Sometimes the EL will respond with his or her first job they had out of university. But I'm more interested in beginning with the *very* first job—the time they were eight and had a lemonade stand, or worked as a newspaper carrier, or whatever it happened to be. You want to get all the way down to that level. Our working lives don't begin when we're twenty. Much of our character is shaped earlier, in our adolescent years. As a result, our experiences in those years are rich in information, and what happened then can be very predictive for what will happen in the future. As an added bonus, it's rare that these experiences will have been discussed in this kind of context before. Indeed, when you ask someone to vividly describe the experience, it's far easier to avoid the canned responses that are often given in a more traditional interview processes. The role of the interviewer, then, is that of an empathetic listener who spends 75 percent of the time probing and questioning.

What you want to look for is what motivates the individual. "Why were you attracted to that job? What did you like about it? Why did you leave? What did you learn from it? Did you develop successful relationships? Were there any relationships that didn't work?" Ultimately, you'll uncover the candidate's strengths and weaknesses. You're not going to directly ask, "What was your strength in that situation?" Yet that's what you want to get a handle on. Some types of questions to ask might be, "Why did you create the lemonade stand? What did you like about it? What did you not like about it? If you weren't selling as much lemonade as you wanted to, what did you do?" These questions can be surprisingly revelatory about character and approach. One individual might say, "I couldn't sell any lemonade, so I just shut the whole thing down and didn't get another job until I was out of school." But a different candidate might respond, "I moved the stand to a busier location, and I made enough money to buy myself a bicycle." That's the kind of EL you're looking for! That's how conversations like this, which reveal successes, failures, and reactions to both, offer patterns. Over the course of their sharing with you, you can really get a sense of the individual's character and what drives him.

The content of the experience (the "What" in the selection pyramid) is actually far less important than what they did with the experience. For example, a prospective lawyer who worked in a mailroom of a law firm in order to put a legal firm on his résumé, but did nothing with it, is dramatically different from someone who took a job in construction and ended up taking responsibility for mediating between crews and management. Likewise, sometimes outstanding "on-paper" achievements can reveal terribly poor interpersonal skills.

This kind of conversation can be helpful on another level. The

EL may view it as a tremendous opportunity or as a threat. Those who view it as the former will share openly and appreciate the inquiry. In fact, the level of interest demonstrated on behalf of the SL in the interview above is uncommon and frankly unforgettable in the EL's eyes. It's viewed as a courtesy and privilege.

In contrast, individuals who have gotten their success solely by powering their way through (command, control or coercion), politics (who they knew), or through being a prima donna, might be wary of an inquiry like this and be more defensive or guarded. That's actually helpful for you—how someone responds to this line of questioning can be just as revealing as the specifics of what they say. This approach also gives you a much deeper sense of the individual than just looking back on a particular project that the person did for you last year, thus greatly reducing the what-have-you-done-for-me-lately bias discussed above.

We're looking for the greatest long-term view possible. The foundation of long-term success (or lack of it) was laid down for this candidate over time. What have they done in the long term, throughout their work lives? What will they be capable of, going forward? Anyone can have a great project, get some breaks, happen to get the right team, and look like a star. Or maybe the person was a star, but the wrong people were on the team, or they did not have adequate resources and things blew up. Short-term bias can choke off great careers before they begin. Looking back all the way to the lemonade stand gives a highly useful depth to the SL's understanding of a candidate.

So now you've got all these different tools: assessments, reference checks, performance reviews, calibration meetings, and the most important, personal work histories. These tools, in combination, create real effectiveness to select the right people. It's all about informing your intuition to make the right judgment.

Re-Selection

Let's talk about re-selection. Let's say you've selected an EL and put them in a particular role. It doesn't mean they're going to be in that role forever. And it doesn't mean the role is necessarily going to continue to be the same as time passes. So re-selection is about going back and taking a new look, re-evaluating the EL and her efforts. SLs need to be doing that with their teams on a consistent basis. They need to be asking, "Joe in Accounting is one of our key players. Is he still aligned with the job? Is his skill set still aligned with what his role demands?" Let's say he was brought into the role to initiate a change. Now that the change has been implemented, is he the one to maintain it? Is he still in the right role? In other words, we're talking about a continual process of evaluating the fit between the talent, experience, and desires of your ELs on the one hand and the needs of the organization on the other.

This need for regular re-selection is compounded by the fact that corporate success isn't necessarily about climbing the corporate ladder anymore. Since the corporate hierarchy is much flatter in many organizations, most opportunities are not clearly vertical but horizontal-ish, and a career path is more lattice-like than ladder-like. When organizations were taller, when change was less frequent, and when the pace of change wasn't as quick as it is today, career paths were much more predictable. So the SL must be proactive in terms of making sure that the ELs are where they belong—and they cannot wait for the ELs to prompt that conversation.

Section III

Develop and Leverage Your Emerging Leaders

Introduction

The Elements of Performance: The Human Capital Formula

Thomas Davenport wrote a book called *Human Capital,* in which he defines the factors that impact the value of human capital in organizations. He literally created a formula that maps out the key ingredients that comprise human capital—in essence, the value employee(s) create. For the sake of our discussion, I've substituted general human capital with the capital of Emerging Leaders specifically. The formula looks like this:

EL (Achievement/Value) = (Ability + Behaviour) x Effort x Time

Basically, the formula says this: if an organization wishes to leverage the ROI from its ELs (or any other employee population), there are a number of factors that can be influenced to do so—the ability, or capability, of its ELs; how they achieve their results (behaviour); how hard they work (effort); and how long they stay with the company (time). If any one or more of these factors is increased, the value the individual provides increases as well. Both "ability" and "behaviour" can be grown and changed to various degrees. And an organization can foster greater amounts of discretionary "effort" and encourage employees to spend more "time" with the company. How, as an SL, can you increase your

EL's ability and foster behaviour with a greater impact, more quickly? How can you create an environment where ELs naturally want to contribute their knowledge and skills in new ways and want to stay longer?

Let's begin this analysis by asking what organizations bring to the table. First, they offer the employee cash—a salary. Second, they offer the employee culture (what it's like to work at a particular company). Third, the organization offers career learning opportunities, as in opportunities for promotion, opportunities to upgrade skill sets, and opportunities to take on different roles within an organization.

The EL comes to the table with knowledge, talents, and skills, and as mentioned above, the organization offers cash, culture, and career opportunity. So how do we come together so that both win and win big, as opposed to each one trying to outsmart the other? How do you create a highly proactive, productive, and profitable relationship between Me, Inc. and the company? That's the subject of the balance of this book.

8

Principle 1: Create Partnership

The old dynamic in the business world was the ongoing tension between employers and employees, where each sought to get the most out of the other side while providing the least. It's characterized by that little sign you sometimes see in people's cubicles or workspaces—"You expect me to show up here for eight hours *and* work?"—and the popularity of the cartoon Dilbert. The mobility of the current workforce, combined with the impending transition of leadership, is ushering in what I believe will be a new age of employment relationships, in particular for ELs. It will be an age of partnership: how we can work together to create value for all of us. Disappearing is the old employer "do as I say, you're my employee" model—and it will disappear with your ELs first. After all, as Me, Inc.'s, they're no longer employees in their eyes, they're suppliers! Many organizations have paid lip-service to this approach of partnership. To illustrate this, I want to share with you a tale of two auto manufacturers and how they treat their suppliers.

Toyota has a 500-year business plan, believe it or not. They have a plan that looks five centuries into the future, to determine where the company needs to be. Okay, 500 years into the future—there's only so much you can predict. And the further out you go, the fuzzier things get. But the company actually has a business plan that reaches out all the way to the year 2500. Indeed, the first principle of fourteen found in Jeffrey Liker's book *The Toyota Way* is "Make decisions based on the long-term impact vs. the short-term impact." This long-term mentality shows up not only in Toyota's relationships with its employees but extends to their suppliers and is embodied in their eleventh principle, which centres around "developing their suppliers" (think "Me, Inc."). Within this commitment, they work together to solve problems and challenges, because everyone's in it for the long haul. In essence, they create a dramatically different sense of partnership.

Let me contrast Toyota's partnership mentality, which allows them to look at the (really) long term, with that of the ailing American auto manufacturer, General Motors. What follows took place a few short years before the economic fallout of 2008. I work with a company that supplies parts for GM. A few years ago, an agreement was reached between GM and the supplier, and both parties signed for a particular part for a number of years. Periodically, however, when payment arrives from GM, it comes in for an amount less than what was agreed upon. GM decides to make a price adjustment without initiating a conversation to discuss why the change is needed. They unilaterally decide to reduce the price they're willing to pay. Because they have so much economic power, they can get away with it, and the parts suppliers are forced to eat the loss. This is a short-term approach that leaves suppliers feeling resentful about doing business with GM and dispels any sense of partnership. Apparently, this practice of GM isn't an isolated one.

This mistrust shows up in other ways as well. When GM comes in for their customary plant tours, they criticize the plant manager for a host of things and search for ways to find money from them—if cycle times are faster than the supplier quoted, there's a saving there; if the supplier doesn't have as many people on shift as was quoted because efficiencies were found, they question that too, and ask for price reductions . . . and on and on it goes. It's come to the point that, when GM comes for visits, they actually *slow the plant down and go back to less efficient methodologies,* just so they can keep the savings they've earned. And of course, if there is an increase in raw material prices affecting the supplier's ability to profit, the typical response would be, "Oh, that's not our problem, it's in the agreement." Take, take, take was GM's approach. Is it any wonder GM (and their suppliers) are in as much trouble as they are, and the suppliers' workers literally cheer (no kidding) when Toyota representatives enter the plant?

When Toyota comes in to perform customary plant tours of the supplier, they send one or two people, ask a number of questions, and offer suggestions about how they might improve cycle times or reduce inventory. If they come back on the next visit and find that the supplier has implemented a change, they're thrilled! They openly share process improvement information they've learned from countless other suppliers around the world. They want to develop their suppliers. Oh, and by the way, the productivity (and financial) gains the supplier realizes are the supplier's to keep. Toyota is committed to developing its suppliers. They know it's more important to have the suppliers be strong, stable, and profitable than to walk across the street for someone else's five-cents-a-part cheaper prices.

Contrast that with GM's plant tour, where a dozen or more people arrive, and you see the difference between these companies: one seeks partnership, and one does not. Interestingly, this mentality trickles down to the plant floor. General Motors and Ford actually offer their suppliers great prices on cars. Local dealerships hold special events where employees of suppliers can come in and purchase cars at deep discounts. According to my client, very few people take advantage of the offer to buy vehicles, despite the truly excellent deals they are offered. And yet, when Toyota subsequently did the same thing and created car event days at local dealerships with similar purchasing incentives, a groundswell of purchasing ensued. That sense of enmity and lack of trust evidences itself in terms of car-buying decisions on the part of people who know nothing about the specifics of dealing with GM. Those same employees who turned down the opportunity to buy GM cars at great prices flock to the Toyota dealerships when afforded the same choice.

Of course, there are many factors that explain this behaviour, one of which relates to the overall quality of the vehicles. But it's impossible to deny the impact of the long-term versus short-term mentality that the companies display, as evidenced in the desirability of their products.

Ideally, you no longer have to be at war with your employees. That's one of the positive changes in the business world today. Yes, the progressive ones are a Me, Inc., but they are looking to contract with (but not merge with) your You, Inc. and turn the relationship into a partnership called "Us, Inc."

Employers can no longer look at their key workers with a short-term attitude of "I will squeeze out of you what I can," as the domestic automakers have been doing with their supply chain for years. Nor can they rely on the "*laissez faire*" approach of seeing what happens. It's really about shifting to the behaviours a longer-term perspective provides and really working together proactively as partners, as in the Toyota model. So that's the premise of what we're going to look at here: how to shift to the longer-term perspective, to proactively partner with ELs, and to create that Us,

Inc. and enjoy its benefits. The following are some specific practices to help you realize Principle #1: Create Partnership.

Practice 1: Become a co-creator of the EL's future.

One of the most important things you, as an SL, can do to foster that sense of Us, Inc. is to focus on the future and not just getting the next project or initiative out the door. Indeed, as an SL, you can build on an innate human tendency to look toward the future. Whatever is or is not in that future has a dramatic impact on how the EL responds *today.*

Here's an example. We've all gone on holidays at some point or another. I remember in 1999, my wife and I wanted to do something really special with the changing of the Millennium. We had a lot of fun coming up with all the crazy things we could do. We talked about it for months as we looked at all our options. In the end, we booked a trip to New Zealand so that we could be some of the first on the planet to see the first sunrise of the new Millennium. When we created a future of "the millennium in New Zealand," it started impacting us—the moment we thought of it, not ten months later when we finally went. We couldn't help but look forward to it. It often came up in conversation with friends and family; we read more travel books on the area. I even asked for a bungee jump to celebrate my birthday while we were there. We were excited. Sure, we enjoyed our four weeks away, but the anticipation and excitement of the holiday started almost immediately.

The converse scenario happens if the future goes uncreated between the organization and the EL; it's left dangling as "anybody's guess." I'll give you an example from my own coaching work of "anybody's guess." I was working with an organization employing an EL who was beginning to feel stale and wanted to shift her career. She confided to me that she was thinking about a career change that involved working on various boards as a director. Her goal was to construct a career solely out of serving on boards—her passion—and she told me candidly that she was thinking of leaving her company to focus on just that. Her Senior Leader was completely unaware of her intentions.

Now, this next part might seem counterintuitive, but bear with me. I knew this was an opening for action for her, and together we created a five-year plan that would allow her to exit the company in five years; in the meantime, she would work on more and more projects that would train her for the career goal of serving full-time on boards. Why would I work with an EL and co-create a plan with her to leave in five years? The answer is that this person would have left anyway, likely in the next six months—or worse, she might have stayed, sitting around, coasting, bringing less and less energy to her work.

After creating her career objectives, she shifted almost instantly. When we first met, despite her talents, she was disengaged, bored, and thought there was no opportunity in her organization for her to develop or display her talents. What's happened since—and this is what's so brilliant—is that she is having conversations with her boss and her boss's boss about what she wants to do in the organization. She is creating opportunities and stepping up to a whole new level in her role and her leadership. By the time this book appears, she will have applied her talents and will be running a major national initiative in the organization in an area that she loves, all while building a skill set that may allow her to leave, if she chooses.

Now she's completely engaged with her work, because the future we co-created completely lines up with what she wants to do with her life going forward. The work that she is now performing for the company has a direct and visible impact on her plan's bottom line. And the irony is that after five years, she may not want to go elsewhere, because she is now so engaged and she's able to use her talents to the greatest degree. This all comes back to one of the points I've stressed throughout the book: your ELs want to be engaged and are constantly looking for ways to make themselves more attractive to the outside world. The more attractive you make them look, the more likely they're going to want to stay with you. That's the power of co-creating futures together.

Many organizations have individuals like the person I just mentioned. Failing to take advantage of the EL's deepest desires for growth is like leaving money on the table. It sometimes frustrates me when I see SLs managing ELs right out of the organization, because the SLs are unaware of the EL's real talents and their hunger for growth and the opportunity to serve. But it's not that hard to take someone from "I'm ready to leave. I'm bored. I'm not so sure I want to be here anymore" to someone who is capitalizing on their deep company knowledge and working to build a bigger future, both for the company and for his or her own career. The lesson: When developmental opportunities are matched up with what the Emerging Leader wants to create, you now have an unstoppable force instead of a bored employee with one eye on the want ads.

So what stops SLs from engaging in these simple conversations about the future that make such a difference? As an SL, you don't always know what's next and you don't want to promise things you can't deliver. This is often a big stopping point for SLs in having these kinds of conversations. Don't let it be. The ELs don't necessarily need hard promises. They understand business is unpredictable, but they want to be at the table with you in having the career conversation. The fact that the conversations are happening is more important than the actual content of the discussions. Keeping the dialogue of what the EL wants and what the organization wants and needs provides the opportunity to create these futures, even incrementally, and gives both parties something to work toward.

Secondly, there may be a concern that the organization just may not have what the EL wants and needs. "If we can avoid the conversation, then perhaps the EL won't say anything," the SL might say to himself. Delay tactics can creep in on the SL's part because it's simply easier to avoid the topic of the future than to deal with it. The uncertainty and lack of communication creeps into the SL-EL relationship and frustration and mistrust begins. That tactic may work in the short term, but ultimately, it's a losing strategy (and with a lack of genuine open dialogue, it is often not based in reality). As Me, Inc. employees, ELs regularly evaluate their "investment" in the organization; that's just the way things are in today's environment. Would you rather they do that evaluation alone, or with you at the table providing input and shaping opportunities? We all appreciate the outcome of straightforward, honest conversations that a partnership can bring. Sometimes these can be awkward conversations to have, but they are critical indeed to creating partnership. It's also why we offer some of the best training to help SLs define and create futures with their ELs.

To go back to the Toyota versus GM analogy, Toyota meets annually with its chief suppliers. Toyota's people ask, "How is this relationship working? Where are we going? What's happening?" They are co-creating a future with their suppliers instead of seeing them as an adversary. This is the mindset that SLs need to adopt in order to partner with their ELs. Co-create the future with your ELs on a consistent, continuous basis. These sorts of formal conversations shouldn't happen just once a year, they should happen every quarter. What have we done this quarter? What have you learned? How is it going for you? Where are we going? This is a continual, ongoing inquiry that needs to take place between the SL and the EL.

Certainly, money is an important motivator for ELs, as it is for anyone who goes to work. But for ELs, it's not just about the money, as we have discussed. It's also about growth and learning opportunities. Other things may come up in these conversations as well; indeed they can and do go in many directions, depending on the employee. Here are some things you might hear:

Many ELs will want to talk about how they can further develop their position with the company. You'll find they're eager to initiate those dialogues.

Others simply need recognition for accomplishments, or will voice needs that you might not have considered.

Some need more career clarity. They're not sure about what to do or where to go next in terms of their professional experiences.

The bottom line: these conversations uncover what's important to the employee. The dialogues may well be uncomfortable at first, if you haven't done this before or aren't used to relating to employees in this way. But the important thing is to reach out and begin the conversations—it may take a few of them for the employee to open up. Start small. It may be a fifteen-minute conversation at first. That's okay, just get started and keep going.

Enterprises exist today in a world that I would describe as "partner or perish." Unless you're going to partner with your key people, it's going to be increasingly difficult to retain them. Since you've spent all this time and energy selecting them, it makes sense to spend time and energy keeping them onboard and engaged. And one key thing that makes them happy is the opportunity for growth. Which leads us to our next practice . . .

Practice 2: Create developmental heat.

You may recall the introduction of Me, Inc. earlier in the book and our discussion of the fact that ELs increasingly think of themselves as professional service providers. Creating developmental opportunities with your ELs has a clear and direct impact on the assets of Me, Inc. *Developmental opportunities are the crucial bridge between the EL's needs and the needs of the company.* And although it may seem completely counterintuitive to keep your ELs marketable by developing their skill sets, there are four clear benefits to creating these opportunities:

1. Increased skills mean an increased ability for the EL to add value beyond the short term.
2. Greater engagement of the EL with your organization. What EL wouldn't want to work with a company that provides great opportunities to grow and learn?
3. Tangible ROI and business results while the individual learns—not just theoretical knowledge that sits on a shelf somewhere.
4. As an SL, you—yes, you—earn a reputation as a talent developer. Birds of a feather flock together; ELs talk and network with other ELs. Talent-developer SLs are highly attractive, sought out and talked about by the best ELs. You will start attracting a better calibre of employee to your division, because they know you'll help them.

At the end of the day, it's a win for all parties. So let's talk a little more about what you need to look out for in creating these opportunities with your ELs.

The first thing to keep in mind is that *people learn best by doing*. The best classroom is reality. I've asked many executives to look inside their organizations and consider their own Senior Leaders and ask how they got where they are. And what many find is that the people at the very top of their companies had no particular formal background, education, or career path. They simply had a wide variety of experiences that allowed them to grow. They learned by doing. So the most important thing you can do to increase the ability of your ELs is give them as many opportunities as possible for them to learn by doing. Seventy percent of learning happens on the job. Twenty percent of learning happens through people, when one person tells another about how to handle a particular situation (bosses, mentors, colleagues) or when someone demonstrates how *not* to do something (the bad boss, mistakes of others, etc.). And the last 10 percent happens in training.

Many companies make the mistake of reversing this ratio, providing too much classroom training at the expense of on-the-job training. It's true that if someone messes up in a classroom setting, the cost to the company is low, whereas if an EL makes a mistake in the real world, the costs can be extremely high. But your people won't grow at the same rate unless they have the opportunity to learn by doing, and that includes making mistakes. Training that offers on-the-job learning opportunities becomes a highly leveraged investment: not only do the employees learn, but they have to consciously apply the learning to reality *and* they create ROI directly from the learning. It's a double bonus—learning and ROI, instead of learning and "hope for the best."

Indeed, the importance of the "learning by doing" principle is challenging the very relevance of MBA programs in higher education and their ability to develop leaders. Leaders must be people who not only know what to do theoretically, but who can actually initiate change and get the job done in real-world scenarios. Essentially, the MBA industry is coming up against an uncertain future because they haven't kept up with the changing business environment. Now many of them are looking at revamping their programs to create a much greater focus on practical application and "soft skills" rather than theory.

The December/January 2008 issue of *Academy of Management Journal* reported on ten scholars' criticism of the entrenched practice of business school research. Warren Bennis of USC's Marshall School of Business went so far as to say that research has so little connection to business reality that MBA programs are "institutionalizing their own irrelevance." Many feel that leadership simply can't be learned in a classroom environment.

Business school curricula are still largely based on the command-and-control management model, created when corporations were large, vertical bureaucracies. Managers spent entire careers with a single, limited job description, and they stayed in that function without much involvement of—or even awareness of—the business as a whole. As we've discussed before in this book, this picture of the business world is becoming increasingly irrelevant. Joel Podolny, the dean of the Yale School of Management, explains it this way: "As organizations have become flatter, those running them are looking for leaders who can see opportunities and address problems that cut across functional boundaries." What it comes down to is finding managers who can think just like Me, Incs.

This means creating "know-how" (practical ability) rather than just "know what" (theoretical knowledge). For many business school graduates there's a gap between knowing and doing, and the only way to bridge that gap is by developing leadership capability through experiential learning. You can't simply open a textbook and memorize soft skills like self-awareness, introspection, and empathy by rote. They only come with practice. And they come much, much faster with the one-on-one involvement of an experienced guide. In MBA programs, this means that faculty members have to forgo the research that has preoccupied them in favour of flexing their developmental muscles. In your organization, it means essentially the same thing: finding a way to balance the day-to-day needs of your organization with the time required to guide and develop your ELs.

In a real work environment, what is sometimes referred to as "action learning" or on-the-job training creates what I call "developmental heat"—which I define as a constructive pressure to learn and perform. The concern that managers have in devoting serious time and effort to the development of their ELs is often the question of payoff for the time invested. Nurturing talent is often viewed as a proposition where the ROI can only be found far in the future. In a world where people shift jobs more rapidly than ever, many SLs tell me that they like the idea of developing their ELs, but they fear that they are simply developing their ELs to succeed at their next employer or with another department, not where they are working right now. In other words, the SLs say, "They're not going to stick around, and I'm not going to get the ROI."

My experience is the opposite—you do get a considerable ROI in the short term when you invest time and care in the growing of your ELs by creating practical, hands-on applications. I believe very strongly in linking training and development to ROI. SLs can create assignments for ELs that serve two functions: they benefit the company in the short term, and they benefit the EL in terms of personal/career development, which pays off in the long term. In many ways, this debate is reminiscent of a question frequently asked of Disney, which spends inordinate amounts of time, money, and other resources training people. The question they frequently hear is, "What happens if you train people, and they leave?" Disney's response: "What happens if you don't train them, and they stay?"

It's worth keeping in mind that the developmental opportunities you are providing for your ELs do not have to be in the form of promotions. It's not about making them vice president so that they have a swanky title on their business cards. Inside flat organizations, there are fewer opportunities to do that sort of thing. Quite frankly, many ELs understand and accept this. When you think about the concept of career from their perspective, they are at least as interested in opportunity as they are in money or promotion, because they know that the deeper their experience, the more value they can deliver, and the more money or choices they will be able to command—either with you or with someone else.

The Senior Leader has the opportunity to think a little differently and to get creative about how to build the assets of their Me, Inc. employees.—their ELs—without necessarily giving them promotions. Perhaps there's a global team being assembled on a particular initiative, and you can put them to work on that global team. Or perhaps there's a product launch coming up; you can put them in charge of launching that new product, even though it is beyond the scope of their normal role. The good news is that you, as the Senior Leader, are not solely responsible for the creation of these projects. Your ELs are most likely bursting with ideas about what they would like to do, if they have the opportunity to openly discuss them. It's not entirely on your shoulders to come up with developmental plans for them. As we talked about earlier in Practice 1: Become a *Co-Creator* of the EL's Future. Usually all you have to do is ask; they almost certainly have ideas of their own.

Another critically important thing for ELs when it comes to on-the-job training, which further enhances that sense of partnership, is variety. For an athlete, cross-training is the key to success. Runners will swim, swimmers will ride a bike, and everyone works on core fitness in order to maximize their success in their given sport. When you do the same form of exercise over and over again, your body gets used to it, and growth diminishes rapidly. Athletes today seek "muscle confusion," whereby the variety of approaches to exercise creates continued growth—because the body has to respond in different ways.

Variety creates growth in the workplace just as it does at the gym. Your Me, Inc.-minded EL is keenly aware of this. *Getting the same year* of experience five times just won't fly with today's EL. Heck, two years can even be a stretch. ELs want the career equivalent of muscle confusion through your offering them a variety of projects and responsibilities on which to work. In so doing, you will be doing the thing that is most important to the EL: broadening their capabilities and thus making them more professionally attractive internally or externally.

I understand that it's not always within the comfort zone of an employer deliberately to make an employee more attractive to competitors. But once again, that's the paradox—the more attractive you can help them look to others, the more attractive you look to them. And that's one way you're able to create that sense of partnership that comes from both sides seeking a win-win. You, Inc. and Me, Inc. can continue to bluff and play their cards close to their chests, or they can become partners, put the cards on the table, and build together. As in the case of Toyota, that's when the long-term future is yours.

For an SL, the question then arises: "If I'm going to provide opportunities for my ELs, what types of opportunities will expand their leadership capabilities the fastest? What will produce the most value?" What follows are the opportunities I've seen produce the most "developmental heat":

Characteristics of Potent Developmental Opportunities

i. Success isn't certain and the outcome will be obvious to SLs

- profit and loss accountability
- negotiations
- working with key leaders

ii. Working with new people or groups of people

- cross-functional teams
- problem employees

iii. Increased pressure created

- challenging timelines
- high stakes/big down sides
- increased scope or scale

iv. Influencing people, variables, and activities without direct control

- cross-functional teams
- outside parties
- projects; off-the-job experiences (volunteering etc)

v. Demands a take-charge leadership approach

- building/fixing something
- need to create new direction

Practice 3: Reward initiative rather than punishing mistakes.

When developing ELs, it's important to create an environment for them that allows for the possibility of failure—not constant failure, but making a mistake from time to time. While this may seem an obvious thing to do, it's far less common than you'd imagine. If you are encouraging people to swing out, you have to let them know, and you have to demonstrate through your actions that failure is a part of business.

I once heard about two individuals in an organization given the task of launching an entirely new division. They were given a budget of $20 million, and they totally bombed. The whole thing completely tanked. When the failure became evident, the CEO called them to his office. The two individuals were sitting outside, waiting, thinking, "We're finished. We're going to be axed." That was their mood as they awaited the dreaded meeting. And then they went into the CEO's office and discovered, to their surprise, that he had arranged a party for them!

I'm not suggesting that you celebrate losing $20 million every day. But in this case, the CEO acknowledged that they had taken a big risk, had done all their homework, and had done everything they knew to do—even though the whole thing didn't fly. He was celebrating the screw-up, celebrating the initiative, celebrating the fact that they had swung out the way they did to try to make something happen. Obviously, in addition to the party, there was a great deal of analysis of what happened and why it didn't work. But the message that the rest of the organization received was that if you take chances, work hard, and do everything you can, the company will back you up.

At the end of the day, there are two things that create value in organizations: marketing and innovation. Business, however, gravitates by nature toward repeatable processes and minimizing risk—it's the most economical and profitable approach in the short term. Marketing aside, businesses must innovate and make change to survive in the medium to long term. You've got to let your ELs know that it's okay to screw up. The execs mentioned above weren't being rewarded for failure. Instead, they were acknowledged for their initiative and their attempt to move the organization forward.

Innovation is inherently risky, and yet in today's business environment, innovation is everything. So if you create an environment where people are penalized for their mistakes instead of honoured for taking their chances, innovation won't have any breathing space. In today's business world, it's fundamentally critical to foster an environment where innovation can thrive and where people are given the space to take chances and do things differently. And an EL's manager will have the most direct influence over whether this happens.

Recently, an EL—lets call her Sue—approached me to begin working with her. After many discussions, she managed to get her SL boss to sponsor our coaching engagement. Reluctantly, he agreed. Sue had lost her spark and was seriously considering leaving the organization, but she didn't want to. In our conversations, she saw how she'd contributed to the situation and took responsibility for it. After working through our Accelerated Leader Process and removing some of the perceived limits she was experiencing, she began demonstrating considerable "intrapreneurship" and bringing forward some innovative ideas that would add tremendous value to the organization. She was excited, engaged, and focused.

The only problem was her boss. He dragged his feet on supporting her, despite buy-in from the CEO. He constantly criticized her ideas. Despite her initiative, whatever ideas he thought had merit, he deemed should be led by someone else. Sue's boss wasn't a future co-creator but rather a future-destroyer. His complacent "if it ain't broken, don't fix it" and "you must stay entirely within the box of your role" approach was stifling. At the point of this writing, much of Sue's successes to date were despite the roadblock of her SL manager.

While the lack of support this SL demonstrated might be particularly clear cut, be aware as an SL of the fledgling ideas that are presented and how you or other SLs respond. These ideas are the seeds of change for the future the EL would like to create with the company. Innovation (and leadership) begins as a fledgling, unproven idea. Yes, the ideas are rarely perfect; consider that they will need tending to, watering, and shaping. How that's done by the SL will have a pivotal impact on the growth of those ideas, as well as the value an EL creates for the company and how long they stick around. If ELs are given the right environment, so many exciting things can happen. But they need permission not only to try new things, but to fail.

One of the most common idioms in the business world is the idea of the batting average in baseball—even a .300 hitter is out seven out of ten times at bat. But when we create an atmosphere in which people are not given permission to fail, we're essentially saying to them, "Here's a baseball. Don't strike out. Ever. You'd better hit a home run every time, or your career will suffer." How can innovation thrive in an atmosphere like that? What would happen to a baseball player under pressure to get a hit every time? And yet, that's how many organizations look at giving people opportunities: they only provide opportunities to try something new with the expectation that there's got to be a hit every time. As a result, people will freeze up. They'll second-guess everything they think and everything they do, because the stakes are so high.

On my Web site, I share the case study of a woman named Lisa Everett, an Emerging Leader and a well-respected accountant, who was part of the financial side of a business that had engaged me as her coach. She was highly intelligent and had produced some great things, but her Senior Leader told me that she was still holding herself back. They couldn't figure out why. It turned out that she had extremely high standards, was extremely self-analytical, and was very hard on herself. Even though she demonstrated great leadership, she wasn't really swinging out in her role in terms of setting up accounting systems and making the company operate more efficiently, which was her bailiwick.

During our work together, she took on creating and marketing a whole new line of business. She worked in the financial services field, and because of her analytical accounting skills, it made a lot of sense for her to be connected with it. And yet, she had a young family, she was the primary wage earner, and she felt that she just couldn't afford to make a mistake. If she messed it up, what would happen to her family? In her mind, she became the baseball player who was told, "Don't strike out." She wasn't especially excited about taking on this new opportunity because of the concerns she felt about what would happen if she failed.

It's rare that any SL would assert that if X didn't work out, the EL would suffer "career consequences." But SLs need to be aware that that assumption exists and can hinder the value you capture from ELs. As a result of addressing Lisa's concerns in our coaching, she ended up creating a line of business that, when I last checked, was producing more than $10 million in annual profits, year after year. If we hadn't allayed her concerns about the safety to take risks, it's unlikely that she would have gotten involved with that new product line, and certainly she wouldn't have engaged to the extent she did. This harkens back to the story I told about Google, where the employees are encouraged to spend up to 20 percent of their working day on projects they initiate—because you never know where the next big idea will come from.

Practice 4: Provide work and career flexibility.

Cathy Benko and Anne Weisberg, in their book *Mass Career Customization,* paint a compelling picture of today's workplace and draw attention to the fact that it is largely founded on an outdated premise: the traditional, single-income family structure of the pre-1980s. In 1950, the US Census Bureau reported that 60 percent of families were traditional, single-income earners: a married couple, one person working outside the home, the other not. Careers were linear, and the common expectation was that you had to dedicate your life to your work if you wanted to get ahead. The workplace was created with this traditional family structure as a basis, and it hasn't changed significantly until the recent decades. Today, however, the number of single income households is a meagre 17 percent. Fully 83 percent of today's working families don't fit the basis the current workplace structure was built on.

Nowadays, there is a tremendous need for flexibility that just wasn't required when today's SLs entered the workforce. Telecommuting, flex hours, trading overtime for days off—these things mean the world to ELs. They're not nine-to-fivers by nature. With the proliferation of dual-income households and many interests outside of work, flexibility is of premium value to make their lives, as a whole, work. When you can provide them with flexibility in terms of scheduling, it makes working for you dramatically easier and more attractive.

This need for flexibility is found both on a day-to-day level and also on the levels of the career itself. That may mean they want the opportunity, on occasion in their careers, to step down from the high-flyer list without being penalized. Whether they are expecting a child or running an Ironman, they don't want to have to compromise their life goals in order to achieve their work goals. If you create an environment where career advancement isn't linear, but more lattice like, making a lateral or slightly "down" move becomes accepted. Then the flexibility to create careers that better fit the ebbs and flows of the ELs' lives becomes possible. This might look like stepping down from the high-flyer list and taking a smaller, less demanding role temporarily, where the workload or schedule are more suitable. If you can create these opportunities for ELs to customize their careers without long-term career penalties, you're giving them exactly what they want and, again, making yourself highly attractive as an employer.

ELs want (and need) flexibility, both in their jobs and in how they progress in their careers.

9

Principle 2: Cultivate Open, Transparent Communication

Your ELs want transparent communication. They want leaders who are honest and open, both in what they share and what they're willing to hear. They want to know about the big picture, the vision of the division or company, what the intensions of the company are, and how their roles and accountabilities fit into it.

Practice 1: Eliminate command-and-control mentalities.

As I've mentioned previously, most North American corporations founded more than a generation or so ago were built on the command-and-control, hierarchical model of management. Their business culture has been steeped in this mentality for decades. Chances are, this is the kind of culture in which you were developed as an SL. The younger you are—if you're an SL who is 45–55 years of age, for example—the lesser the degree to which you'll have experienced and been influenced by this.

Much has been written over the years about new management practices. Nevertheless, the older you are as an SL, the more likely you'll naturally find yourself slipping into command-and-control habits as a default setting, simply because it's what you likely experienced in your formative years as a manager. Maybe you were just as uncomfortable with this model as your ELs are today, but because it was the model embraced by your company's culture, you had to emulate it or at least were influenced by it—because that was how it was done. As I've said throughout the book, you climbed up a ladder, while ELs today are climbing along a lattice. The top-down, command-and-control practices, which were rarely about transparent communication between boss and subordinate, won't sit well with today's generation of ELs.

At the extreme, command-and-control practices are characterized by inflexibility, and they reward compliance. Because direction comes from a few sources at the top, there is a tremendous amount of pressure on command-and-control managers to appear infallible, to check up on their employees, and to demand rather than earn their respect—but not necessarily to return that respect. They are also under pressure to reward employees who don't question or challenge their authority, especially publicly. The manager must make all the decisions and dictate the strategy with little or no input from the people reporting to him. Once a project begins, he must micromanage it and know exactly what is going on at every stage.

As you know, in today's fast-paced and complex business world, micromanagement is increasingly inefficient. It has become literally impossible to know and understand everything that is going on at every moment. At the same time, of course, managers still remain accountable for their team's work. This presents a paradox for command-and-control managers, and unfortunately, they simply cannot stick to old methods and expect to function in today's climate. Not only does the time and complexity barrier make command-and-control management unfeasible, but the next generation of employees simply won't work under it—and they don't have to.

If a company is still heavily run in a command-and-control manner, there are really only three ways you can expect to see ELs respond. They'll request an internal transfer, leave the company altogether, or worse yet, allow their good ideas and solid input to be squashed and wasted, creating a vicious cycle of resentment and lack of productivity. They're not interested in being told what to do, and they demand a more collaborative approach. They want to know what end result is expected and what you want to create, and they don't want to be micromanaged and given all the steps to get there. They want to be empowered to create results and not managed on a smaller scale, given all the puzzle pieces in order to complete the picture. They want to figure it out for themselves. When you replace command-and-control with a sense of autonomy—bolstered by transparent, effective communication—you're singing your ELs' song.

Practice 2: Treat people and performance fairly—not equally.

The next thing that makes ELs sit up and take notice in a positive way is when they sense that you are treating performance fairly, not necessarily equally. Nothing will tick off a go-getter-style EL, who's out there kicking butt and doing a great job, more than being evaluated in a manner that's similar to his peers who haven't been able to produce the same results. You can no longer compensate or reward people in lockstep or based primarily on seniority. I've had multiple situations in which an EL is the newest person in a department where some of the people have been there for twenty years. And the EL notices that some of the people in the department are underperforming but have more seniority, and therefore more job security and higher pay.

If the new EL receives a performance review indicating that she's been doing a great job, showing initiative, doing cool things—but she's being lumped in with the more senior stragglers—for the results-oriented employee, that's a complete de-motivator. ELs need to know that you are honouring their specific job contributions in a manner consistent with their efforts and that you are not just rewarding seniority over success.

It's important to emphasize that this doesn't necessarily mean paying people more. Often, in the case of wage bands for particular roles, there is only so much room for a manager to play with in rewarding an employee. But rewards in the form of bonuses and pay increases aren't the only tools available. There are the other practices mentioned earlier in the book, such as flexibility and learning opportunities. And recognition—coming formally, informally, or in the industry—is another useful way of distinguishing performance.

Performance needs to be differentiated. ELs are saying, "If you're going to lump me in with everybody else while I'm working my buns off and really showing commitment and ambition and discretionary effort, that's not going to work for me." Your ELs don't expect to be treated equally. They expect to be treated fairly.

One way of distinguishing the contributions of your ELs is to acknowledge their placement on the "napkin list." Whether an organization has a formal succession planning process or none at all, there is, at minimum, a "napkin list," an informal inventory of high-potential people to evaluate and keep an eye on. Quite often, the list is kept secret for fear of raising the EL's expectations or turning off people who don't make the list.

Like any business, a Me, Inc. wants to know where they stand with their customers. If you've got their name on a napkin succession list, tell them. Don't make them guess, because they live in a world where communication is everything. Indeed, the generation under 40 today is defined in terms of their need to communicate.

They have the most powerful communication tools ever created and their access to information is unprecedented.

When we talk about open and transparent communication, we're also talking about your responsibility as an SL to communicate to the EL where he stands in terms of the company's future. Does he have a future in the company? Is he on the napkin list? Let him know, because if you don't, he may mistake your failure to communicate for a lack of interest on your part in his career. And for ELs, that doesn't work.

Their need for feedback also ties into the performance imperative that managers must—on a regular basis—go "naked" about how they're feeling about an individual's performance. Sometimes this is called "The Ultimate Management Irony" (UMI), pronounced "YOU-ME," where leaders often fail to bring real honesty to performance conversations for fear that they'll hurt the employee's feelings or negatively impact their attitude going forward. It is remarkable how many stories I've heard about dissatisfied employees telling other non-boss managers, "I wish my manager would tell me how I'm doing. I have no clue what he's thinking." So you have one party wanting information, the other party is withholding, and it's being withheld because the second party believes that the first doesn't really want it.

If you have a robust succession plan, sometimes what's missing is actually communicating that plan to the individuals on the list. Failing to let your EL know that he is on the list leads to what I call the "on bended knee prayer implementation phase," where the organization has these grand plans for individuals, but they've kept the plans from the individuals. The "on bended knee" phase comes out in two ways:

1. Hoping (or naively assuming) that the individual will stick around until the next opportunity arises, or

2. Assuming that individuals will jump when they are approached for the first time about an opening in the organization.

Both situations occur because of little (if any) communication with the ELs about their potential and because of the absence of any clear, expressed indication of the intentions of the company. Can you imagine the lost productivity that comes during the time when the person doesn't know about the potential you see for their future? They could be jazzed and motivated beyond measure if they knew! Failure to communicate wouldn't work in a relationship or a marriage for long, and it certainly won't work in this setting. Let your ELs know they're on the list. And ask them where they want to go.

If you talk to your EL about your plans for her, you may find that she has a presumption about a particular promotion or next step in the career ladder or lattice in your organization. Perhaps she believes that there is a great deal of travel associated with the position, or there are other responsibilities that might interfere with her family life, or her plan to run that Ironman. It's vital for you, as an SL, to engage your EL in conversation and find out what she believes about the next job she's likely to have at your company. Is it something she wants? Is there a better fit elsewhere in the organization?

In the absence of these kinds of conversations, as human beings we are wonderfully creative at coming up with stories about what's going on. If an EL is producing decent results and/or showing initiative, but their requests for these types of conversations remain unanswered or the company doesn't initiate them, it's natural to interpret the silence in a negative way and assume that you simply don't care about her career growth. She may believe that there aren't any opportunities or that her work may not make it onto the succession radar. At that point, thoughts about searching for a new job can begin. Indeed, believe it or not, it is often the most sensationally talented people who create the most negative stories in their heads about themselves and how others see them. The old belief that the best people are often hardest on themselves still holds true.

Alternately, if the organization is giving ELs development opportunities without acknowledging that those assignments are developing them for future roles, ELs can wonder why the heck they're being sent to work on projects that don't seem relevant to where they want to go. It's a little like an arranged marriage—it works in traditional cultures, but not for people whose context is the broader world. I'm sorry to say this, but your ELs don't feel married to your organization. They feel free to date outside the relationship! The only way to nip that in the bud is to communicate with them about where they want to go in your organization. Otherwise, they'll always wonder and you risk having them look elsewhere as a result.

There is a common concern about selecting the high-performers without alienating the rest. If it isn't done properly picking select employees for succession related development like leadership training can raise a concern of favouritism. This concern leads to the closed-door approach described above. To avoid the perception of favouritism and the backlash that can ensue, the process must be transparent. Create a clear criteria for getting on "the list." Making the criteria well-known and having a formal process will reduce the chances of negative reactions.

In addition, give your ELs multiple chances to take the reins of new leadership roles. As I've highlighted earlier, there may be a number of life-stage development factors (kids, marathons, etc.) that could preclude them from jumping on the first leadership opportunity that's presented. Providing multiple chances to join the leadership group will help ensure that their readiness matches well with the opportunity.

Get rid of the napkin. Create a real, formal list and clear criteria for getting on it. Be open with your ELs about where they're at and what's needed to get on the list (if they're not on it). At a minimum, for goodness sakes, communicate with those who are on it. Communication is one of the most effective and underutilized retention and engagement tools available.

Practice 3: Create tangible performance and development plans.

Here's the good news about this practice: if you've already gotten started on "Principle 1: Create Partnership" and begun to foster greater partnership with your ELs, you're way ahead of the game. Creating tangible performance and development plans is much less about creating a piece of paper than it is about having meaningful conversations.

That said, I do advocate having *tangible* plans—documents that clearly delineate, in print, the path you and your EL plan to take in terms of performance and development. But the process of creating those documents is of infinitely more value than the documents themselves. And that process is all about open, mutual dialogue. So, keeping in mind that the process (the conversation) is more important than the destination (the plan), I'll first describe what I mean by "performance and development plans," and then we'll take a closer look at the process of creating them.

The performance plan. This plan is fairly immediate and oriented toward business results. It focuses on the relatively short term, usually a twelve-month period. Essentially, it answers the question: "What are we going to be accomplishing in the next year?" It lists specific objectives for that time frame and describes how an individual can work toward accomplishing or contribute to the accomplishment of those objectives within the structure of their current job description. It might outline steps toward the goal, and it might refer to compensation.

The development plan. As opposed to the performance plan which deals primarily with direct results *for the business*, the development plan focuses on developing the capacity of the EL. As Me, Incs this plan is *crucial* for ELs because it essentially equates to a personal marketing plan for the EL. Remember, in the EL world, skills plus experience equals marketability which, in turn, equals security. The plan typically encompasses a larger time frame, usually stretching as far into the future as two or three years. It addresses the question of where an individual wants to go in your organization and what opportunities they're looking for to keep them engaged and to create more value for you. It might refer to specific business objectives; it might discuss short-term goals (to be accomplished in the next quarter, six months, or year); and it might refer to compensation. But these appear in the plan only as they relate to the individual's development. If, for example, the development plan addresses an individual's goal of beginning to manage a certain type of project three years down the road, it might include short-term goals like developing a necessary skill-set within the next six months. In that sense, it might resemble or even have some overlap with a performance plan. But the important thing is that the business results it addresses also will have some developmental significance for the individual.

The process of creating these plans in document form is almost like a formalization of the partnership conversations I've been advocating until this point. You'll already be asking your ELs what *their* goals are as part of co-creating a future together; creating these plans provides you with a tangible outcome for some of those conversations. You might be used to thinking of plans as something you create and hand off to your subordinates, like a written form of delegation. By contrast, what I'm suggesting is that you and the EL create these plans together, as a next step in the open partnership you've already begun to foster. Each of you will individually create your version of the plan and then you'll come together to build a mutual plan based on both parties' input. This way, the EL has ownership of the path he will be heading down; he can think of it as a plan for himself as well as for the company. It simply creates more buy-in as a natural outcome of the process.

It's a win-win situation. Both plans can provide you with a clearly outlined process for reaching certain goals within your organization, but at the same time, your EL will be able to provide input to ensure that the plans are not one-size-fits-all. He'll be able to make suggestions that keep the organization's needs in alignment with the roles he may or may not want in the company or the flexibility he might need for his personal life. Creating these plans also affords you the opportunity to provide context, to ensure that the EL understands how his tasks fit into the overall direction of the division or company. The more the EL can link his performance results to an overarching goal, the more likely he is to remain engaged.

The conversation will be much easier if the two of you are already engaged in open dialogue, so that you both have a shared and honest understanding of what opportunities are feasible for the EL. Creating a plan provides a structure in which you can ensure that each party is on the same page in terms of how ready the EL is for a given project or responsibility. But the success of the plan hinges on each individual's ability to express himself honestly and clearly. That may mean delivering awkward news. But that will be infinitely easier if you're already working in a partnership.

The process of building these plans together will involve a lot of asking and not a lot of telling on the part of the SL. It's not about delineating for the EL where he's going and what he needs to be doing. It's about both parties asking each other, "What do you want? What could work? How can we get there?" At some point, the two of you will have to reach a consensus about a specific direction, but the point is that, through open dialogue and mutual input, the horizon broadens. The possibilities are wide open, as opposed to limited by a single vision and set of instructions. It's a much richer level of conversation.

So, what will it look like when you do get specific and nail down a direction? In both types of plans, you'll want to focus on S.M.A.R.T. goals, which you are likely already familiar with in other business contexts. A S.M.A.R.T. goal is Specific, Measurable, Achievable, Realistic, and Timely. Your plan will address each element of the goal: it will describe the final outcome specifically; provide a means by which the accomplishment of the goal can be measured and a time at which this measurement will take place; list steps for achievement; ensure that these steps are realistic, given the individual's and the organization's resource constraints; and outline a time frame for completion.

One of the most critical aspects of a S.M.A.R.T. goal is that its success can be measured and evaluated by clear means. Sometimes this is straightforward and you can use plain numbers or business metrics to determine whether a goal has been reached. Other times, your EL might be working toward a more intangible end, such as leading his team more effectively or being more collaborative. Both types of goals boil down to the core competencies that your organization values, which can be either job-specific or behavioural. The job-specific competencies are easy to identify and measure; they are technical behaviours. For example, can Bob make twenty widgets in a week?

But what if the core competency is a behaviour? Often, it will be. Your organization might place a high value on achievement-oriented employees who are naturally looking to create accomplishment and move the company forward quickly. Or you might need people with strategic business sense. How well does an employee utilize resources to maximize return? Developing others is another behavioural competency. The list goes on and on. We discussed in section II the importance of having a shopping list of what characteristics to look for or cultivate in an EL, so behaviours are definitely things that you're going to have an eye out for at this stage of the game. Often, the tendency with a behavioural goal is to set measurement aside. But in truth, if you don't measure it, there's diminished point in doing it at all. You have to have some means of acknowledging progress or addressing roadblocks.

Here's a simple way of evaluating a behavioural competency. Identify what it would look like in your particular organization if a person were performing at a maximum, ideal level in that competency and assign that level of achievement a "ten" (or whatever score system you deem appropriate). Then describe a mid-level or satisfactory level of achievement, and call it a "five." Not engaging in the behaviour at all would be a "zero." It is also important to note that performance below five may also be for those that are in development and increasing their skill level verses just low performers. Something that helps you describe your expectations for a ten, a five, and a zero, respectively, is to look at the high performers and average performers on your team. What are the high performers doing? Which behaviours make you stop and think, "Hey, they're doing a good job?" Simply put, this will help you create a rubric. The EL needs this information clearly presented so that he can anticipate how he will be measured, who will do the measuring, when that measuring will occur and, of course, what the targets are.

If your organization hasn't already identified these targets or core competencies that it seeks to cultivate, this will be a stumbling block in the creation of your performance and development plans. Identifying core competencies doesn't have to be a mammoth task that you have to pay a consultant a small fortune to undertake. It can actually be done very quickly. A good way to begin is to ask your CEO, "What are the behaviours that you value? What do you love to see people doing in your organization?" If you're part of a large company where you might not have access to the CEO, ask your boss. Make the questions department-specific. Create a list of their answers, and now you've got a tool to help you gauge the core areas of behaviour that are important to your department or company.

If you don't clearly identify these competencies, you'll be doing the EL, and ultimately yourself, a disservice. How can the EL shoot for targets that aren't there? Ultimately, being in the dark like this will lead to a lack of clarity in performance. You won't get the results you want, and your EL will be frustrated or anxious about his job. Mushrooms are the only things that grow in the dark. So shed a little light on the situation, and get clear about and communicate which skills and behaviours are important for the current or future role—for your EL's sake, and for your own.

The final element that is critical for you to include in a performance or development plan in terms of measuring the goals is *timing*. Imagine if a coach arrived on the first day of practice and said, "Okay, guys, our goal is to get to the playoffs, and to do that I want to work on building a strong defense and stretching our forwards' skills a little further." And then imagine he said nothing more about it until playoffs were over. Clearly, it would be a useless exercise. The coach of a team has to be talking about where the team is headed and what needs to be changed at every single practice. It wouldn't make any sense to take a look at performance only once, at the end of the season. Yet this is what happens in the vast majority of businesses today. The same is true for creating a one-year performance plan or a three-year development plan and only reviewing it at the end of the time frame.

The ideal solution, then, is to plan interim reviews at least once a quarter. They don't have to be involved, formal sessions; they could be just sitting down briefly, or for a portion of a regularly scheduled update meeting, reminding each other of where you're headed and asking, "How are we doing as we make our way down that path?" You can also schedule your interim reviews as what I call "after-action reviews." This means that, rather than holding them at the close of specific time periods, you hold them at the completion of specific projects. It's like doing a post-mortem for a project, but the focus is more on the individual rather than the project. Ask your EL, "What happened during the execution of the project? What worked? What didn't work? What did you learn?" Then determine how your EL can incorporate this knowledge going forward and how it related to the goal.

Holding interim reviews or after-action reviews will make the final conversation at the end of the year (or two or three years, depending on whether you're reviewing performance or development) much easier. You haven't been in the dark for six or twelve months at a time, wondering, "When did the EL complete this activity and did he build on that past experience?" If the EL has drifted off target, it won't be a matter of an entire year before you notice and help him get back on course. Instead of sitting down at the customary annual review time and scratching your heads trying to remember what happened, you can focus on building from the experience, moving forward, and creating the next plan.

Technology has come a long way in supporting this process and these conversations. Today, there are a variety of affordable online tools to aid in the process of goal setting, performance reviews, and the like. These systems make it possible for employees to share goals and approaches, accomplishing them as a team. Instead of goals being about a one-to-one relationship discussed between employee and manager, the process can be much more iterative and team oriented. Handling goals in this way helps make the whole goal-setting, goal-management and goal-accomplishment arena more central to an organization and less compartmentalized, which often happens with performance management.

Practice 4: Provide real-time feedback.

As we've touched upon, if you only conduct performance reviews and development conversations once a year, then you're missing incredible opportunities throughout the year to accelerate the growth of your ELs and to leverage the value they produce. By contrast, if you are offering regular feedback and coaching, then the EL is continuously learning about what works and what doesn't work, and they can course-correct as they go instead of waiting a year or more to make a change. That alone has huge value, because otherwise, your EL is operating in the dark and might be getting more and more off course without knowing about it—or alternately, the development objectives may have faded into the background. We started to address all of these issues in the previous section. Now let's take a closer look.

To go back to our central metaphor, you are managing a bunch of Me, Inc. employees. The value they provide to you and your division is a product of how effective they are. As is true for all of us, their effectiveness is accelerated dramatically with feedback—real-time feedback. And as Me, Inc. businesses, ELs are thirsty for it. If you were in a meeting with an EL and they did something that bombed, they'd want to know in real time what went wrong and what to do about it. They don't want to wait months until their next review to hear about it. That's why ongoing conversations providing timely feedback are so important. This works exceptionally well when you've developed a true sense of partnership with your EL, developing a level of trust that allows you to speak your mind and the EL to hear what you have to say. Given the context of partnership, timely feedback is easier to offer and easier to receive.

There is a pitfall to avoid here. It comes when managers confuse the sense of partnership with being friends or simply pandering to the EL's wants and needs. Nothing could be further from the truth. Partnership doesn't imply you have to spoil them in order to accomplish your goal of having a positive relationship. That's not the message we want to send, because that's not partnership.

Instead, we want to create a win for everybody so that your needs as a Senior Leader for getting work done in a timely fashion are met, the future leaders of the company are growing, and your Emerging Leaders' needs—to learn, to be challenged, and to be guided to the next level—are met as well. That doesn't mean that you have to be your EL's best friend. When an SL becomes overly friendly with an EL, hard discussions become even harder. You might need to have a painful discussion with an EL about a failure or a lapse. It could be difficult to give such feedback to an individual if the relationship between the SL and EL is buddy-buddy rather than something more professional.

I won't kid you: it takes commitment and courage to have these kinds of ongoing, performance-related conversations with ELs. Sometimes there's tough news to deliver; it's so much easier to skip over it and just turn to the next e-mail on your Blackberry. But that doesn't give the ELs the feedback they need in order to grow and add more value. Ideally, the communication between the SL and the EL lands as something like, "I'm here to help and I just really want you to be aware of how your XYZ behaviour came across," as opposed to the EL getting either no feedback or critical feedback from an SL and thinking, "They're just putting me down."

Luckily, if you're building on the partnership practices we've been discussing all along, these conversations will become easier and easier. The information I discussed in "Practice 3: Create tangible performance and development plans" will help you institute a system of three to four interim or after-action reviews a year. This system of scheduled reviews provides a context for you to initiate less formal, real-time feedback whenever it's appropriate between reviews. For example, potential EL development areas might be "dealing more proactively with conflict" or "empowering your team." Tying those themes into a formally scheduled meeting or informal chance encounters is extremely useful to bringing them alive and into the forefront of the EL's thinking. I highly advocate simplicity here—one or two core development areas at a time. Feedback is feedback, and it's great whether you already have a review schedule in place or not. But providing feedback in the context of the objectives outlined in the reviews is even better.

What does real-time feedback look like? I often advise SLs to devote the first ten minutes of update meetings to talk about what worked this week, what didn't work, what people learned, and what they didn't learn. These discussions can be as formal as the first ten minutes of a weekly meeting, or they could just simply be a conversation out in the hallway, walking back from a meeting together. The SL might simply ask, "How do you think that meeting went?" Or "What did you think about that meeting? Did you have any concerns about X and Y? What did you think about what so-and-so said? What do you think of their response? What do you think about your response?"

We do have to recognize that Senior Leaders and Emerging Leaders are not always physically located in the same place. It's not always possible for an SL to be with her ELs. Perhaps there's a great deal of travel, or perhaps her reports are spread out among many different satellite offices. SLs should be constantly in the process of gathering information, talking with their reports during update meetings, asking things like, "How's Bob doing over there? What do you think about that issue? How did that meeting go?"

The good news is that real-time feedback doesn't have to take a lot of time, yet it provides an enormous return for the time invested. In addition to simple structures outlined above, it can happen on the fly, and the guidance that the SL delivers can be of immeasurable value to the EL and the organization.

Consider also that, as a manager, you don't have to provide all the support. Informal mentors can be extremely valuable. If your EL is now going to be leading a much bigger project that you aren't directly involved with, ask yourself (and the EL), "Who on the project could be a resource or mentor for the EL during the project? Who knows a lot about this area that may be able to help?" The new mentor's close proximity to the EL during the period is another source of real-time feedback and advice for the EL in that new context. You don't have to do it alone.

My advice about giving feedback boils down to what I learned from an astute leader: "Always be happy, but never be satisfied." It's about being happy with the fact that your ELs are making great progress, but never completely satisfied that there isn't more progress to be made. This will provide you with continual growth and an impetus to nudge them along. If you never appear to be happy with who they are and what they're doing, then you're not creating an environment for growth. It's a little bit like riding a bicycle: you've got to be encouraging rather than discouraging, and there's always room to ride better or faster.

10

Principle 3: Be Responsive

When today's instant communication culture is combined with Me, Inc.'s restless nature and the shifting supply and demand for talent, responsiveness has become even more essential to getting the best from your ELs and keeping them onboard. Responsive in this context means that your SLs proactively listen to what it is that employees have to say and are committed to responding in a timely manner. Responsiveness does *not* mean that everything employees request is done, but a responsive manager and organization communicate clearly what they can and cannot do for their employees in a timely fashion. Responsiveness is about clearly managing expectations and the communication that surrounds that. Some examples of this include:

- Managers provide some form of informal recognition regularly.
- ELs understand the timelines associated with their career paths.
- ELs can talk to their SLs about their careers and receive input and guidance.
- ELs have influence (not control) on how long they stay in their roles or how quickly they advance.

- ELs are asked what type of learning development opportunities would be most valuable to their career goals.
- Performance and development plans are created annually and reviewed periodically.
- The company's succession plan is reviewed and updated on a regular basis, with input from multiple levels in the company.
- ELs' requests for more frequent informal discussions about performance are honoured and encouraged.
- ELs are asked to provide feedback to their SL managers about their performance.
- SLs listen to and respond to ELs' comments and suggestions on their (SL) performance.
- The development of future leaders within the organization is tied to management's compensation.
- SLs provide coaching and support on a frequent basis to their teams.

Section IV

Coaching ELs to Success

11

What You Can't Ignore as a Senior-Leader Coach

We started the conversation in this book at the 30,000-foot level by illustrating the current demographic situation. We then came down to the 20,000-foot level, in which we described the nature of the EL. At 10,000 feet we described how to identify, select, and help guide the careers of the ELs who are expected to add the most value and potentially be groomed for larger roles in the organization. Now, we're coming down to ground level, where we will act on the development plans we've created for your ELs, so that we can be most effective on a day-to-day basis at engaging, retaining, and leveraging them. Everything prior to this moment, really, has been about creating an environment, a context in which performance happens. We're now down to the road . . . where the rubber hits the tarmac and tangible day-to-day value is created.

So far, we've discussed the SL's role with regard to shaping the EL mostly on a macro level: what's most effective at engaging your Emerging Leaders, how you partner with them, what kinds of projects and development opportunities they soak up, and which are important if you want to leverage and retain them. In this chapter, we want to shift our focus to a more micro level, looking at the SL as a coach. We'll now move away from the topic of how to develop the overall career of the Emerging Leader and instead address the question of how an SL actually coaches and supports an EL to offer his or her best performance on a daily basis.

Everything you've done as a Senior Leader on a macro level to address the Emerging Leader's concerns about their careers, aspirations, and where you are going as a company has created a partnership between you and the EL. You've established clear, transparent communication, which the EL reflexively expects from his or her boss. By doing so, you've really set the stage for having a much more influential and productive relationship as a coach with your Emerging Leader. And nothing could be more crucial! In fact, it's well documented.

In their book *First Break All the Rules*, Marcus Buckingham and Curt Coffman describe their study of more than 2,500 business units in twenty-four companies. Ultimately, they found that no single factor influences individuals' desire to stay with or leave a company more than their immediate manager. As an SL, you have the biggest impact on retention, engagement, and value creation when it comes to the ELs who report to you. If you can position yourself positively, you'll be primed to coach them to bigger results for you and a much greater level of success for the organization. But there's a problem.

The Biggest Obstacle to Leveraging and Coaching Your ELs: You're the Boss

Our goal in this chapter is to overcome the natural boss/employee dynamic and instead create clearer, more honest and empowering conversations. It's in these types of conversations that high performance and its associated results can be fostered. Often, I hear about SLs who just begin coaching. They simply ignore this boss/

employee dynamic and pretend it doesn't exist, which leaves the EL confused about how to respond to their superior's sudden shift in behaviour. The SL then wonders why the employee doesn't seem to want to open up to them, despite the fact that they're asking all the right questions.

You cannot get away from the fact that you are that person's boss, and that person cannot pretend that you're not their boss. Ultimately, that hierarchical relationship always exists. As the SL, as the boss, you have the power to determine your EL's salary, where they'll go in the future, where they will rise in the organization, how they will perform the work that you have assigned, and whether they'll keep their job at all.

As a boss, you are responsible for holding the EL accountable for results. You have power over your employee, simply put, and this cannot be ignored. This dynamic is ultimately going to shape and influence the nature of the conversations you have with your EL.

The role of coach is different. A coach's job is to help people develop their skills or capabilities to achieve results. In the role of boss-coach, you have to both set the goal and assist the EL in developing the ability to achieve the goal. As a boss, the fact that you are responsible for the EL's results cannot be overlooked. Indeed, this dynamic needs to be addressed before really effective coaching conversations can occur. If you can manage the coaching function within the overall power dynamic of the boss/employee relationship, you've got it made.

So, for executives who want to coach, we must first acknowledge and distinguish with the EL the roles of boss and coach. Not acknowledging this can lead to two common pitfalls when an SL begins to coach. The first is what I call the "soft boss syndrome," which is a situation where the bottom line results become secondary to developing the employee. It may be in a Senior Leader's nature to enjoy coaching even more than getting results in an organization. If that's the case, you may need to rethink your own career! You simply cannot afford to be looked upon as a "soft boss." Soft bosses, although nice to work for in the short term, don't challenge and get the best from their people. ELs tend to be highly results-oriented; they want to be challenged.

But on the other hand, coaching is also often misunderstood or conveniently used as yet another way to direct people and to tell them what to do. If at one end of the spectrum is the soft boss, you'll find at the opposite end of the spectrum another individual to avoid—what I call the "progressive hardliner." If the progressive hardliner adopts coaching, it's often to use coaching as a license for creating a hard-line, "do it my way" reality for the EL, all dressed up as friendly coaching. It doesn't necessarily happen from a malicious point of view. They may say things like, "Why don't I coach you?" or "I'll coach you on this." But what they're actually doing is just giving a lot more specific direction on a granular level and exerting their control in a disguised manner. So those are the two extremes—the soft side and the hard side. Both of these extremes are to be avoided.

As we discussed earlier, it is extremely rare that an Emerging Leader will "tell all" to a Senior Leader. No matter how great a manager you might think you are (and I've been hired by many), the SL/EL, boss/employee relationship inevitably creates the dynamic in which ELs will hesitate to be completely open with their Senior Leaders about their aspirations, beliefs, and concerns (I know full-well, I hear *all* about these in my calls with ELs). If you're going to be successful as a coach, you'll have to find a way to minimize the impact of the natural tendency of a report to keep their cards close to their vest.

Unless you precede your coaching of the EL with the clear

approach I'll outline below, you will, in all likelihood, waste considerable time and produce poor results. Up to now, your EL has experienced their relationship with you as you, the boss. The EL has seen you setting the direction and doing what bosses do—mainly, exercising authority, power, and control. If you suddenly start coaching, the Emerging Leader may not know what to make of it! They'll be asking, "Do I have a clear direction here? Have I been told what to do, or was this just a suggestion about how to improve my performance? Do I really have a choice in what to do here? How seriously do I take this coaching? What exactly am I supposed to do with it?"

The EL is not the only one experiencing confusion. As the SL, you might be experiencing some uncertainty as well. At any given time, SLs might be wondering, "Should I coach my EL on this given point? Or should I just let it go? When is it useful for me to coach as opposed to providing the traditional guidance and advice a boss is expected to give?" You end up with confusion on both sides, and more often than not, the conversations are avoided altogether as a result.

Before you even start coaching your EL, you've got to make clear that the guidance that you are offering in your coaching role is different from the advice that you give in your role as boss.

External coaches, individuals you bring in from outside your organization, are by nature independent and have an entirely different context to coach within. As a result, they are also lousy coach role models for SLs to follow—more on that in a subsequent chapter. Outside coaches are not attached to the results that their mentees create. They help provide skills and draw out the insights and strategies from their clients (your ELs). When a boss becomes the coach, however, it's a different story. You are responsible for the results, because the outcomes that your ELs create affect how well your department or division performs, and this reflects on your own success within the organization. That's why I stress that it's so important for you to make clear to your ELs when you're wearing your coaching hat and when you're putting on your boss hat.

Before you can even think about putting on your coach hat, however, you have to recognize that there will always be three distinct phases involved in engaging with your ELs:

1. Setting clear performance expectations, or *defining the game*
2. Ensuring commitment, or *getting the ELs engaged in the game*
3. Coaching the ELs who are *playing in the game*

Stages 1 and 2 *must be complete* before you can begin coaching. So let's look at them closely.

Stage 1: Defining the Game

It's often surprising to see how common it is for even seasoned SLs to be unclear in communicating their expectations. Then they scratch their heads about why they don't seem to get the results they want when they coach their ELs. Whether the game is big (a major marketing initiative, for example) or small (like a behavioural pattern you want to shift), you have to be behaviourally specific about your objective and the rules of play. These are the elements an employee needs to understand:

a. What the desired outcome is,
b. Who's participating,
c. By when the project needs to be completed, and
d. How much authority he or she has to make decisions.

Then, have the employee paraphrase the information back to you so that it's clear, and make yourself available for questions and discussion about the objective.

Here's an example: You sit down with your EL and you say, "We need to increase sales 15 percent in XYZ category. You'll be working with Dale, Eric, Sandra in Marketing, and Keith in Product Support *(who)* to reach this objective. I want you to create an action plan *(what)* about how you're going to do this and submit it to me within thirty days *(when)*. The group will have majority vote on each of the recommendations in the final document *(decision-making authority).*"

You've defined the directive, you've explained who the team members will be and how the choice will be made, and you put a deadline on it. Your EL clearly understands what you are asking of her.

Here's another one.

"Starting this week *(when)*, I want you to lead the weekly team meetings. I would like you to create and distribute the agenda a minimum of one day prior to the meeting, open each meeting, keep the team on track during the meeting, and ensure that there are tangible action steps and that appropriate minute notes are taken and distributed *(what)* by the following day *(when)*. Encourage the team to contribute to the agenda. If there are any concerns you can't resolve or there is a dispute about the agenda, please come to me *(decision making authority).*"

Without clear performance expectations or a clear game, it's easy to get off track and misinterpret intention. Imagine the players going onto the football field or the hockey rink without a clear understanding of the intent of the game and the rules to play it by; it would be confusing and frustrating, to say the least. The team coach (you, the SL) would constantly have to stop players from doing the things the game doesn't allow if they didn't understand the rules or intent of the game to begin with. Meanwhile, the other teams who are steeped in clear expectations are running circles around you.

All too often, bosses manage by intuition, using a sort of mind-reading approach to management. While this may work to some degree for yourself with others, don't expect your subordinates to be able to do the same and know what you want and need. The mind-reading approach naturally leads to vague expectations and does not help ELs meet their targets. *Your EL needs a clear statement of purpose, who's involved, what they need to do by when, and what authority they have.*

Setting clear expectations (defining the game) is the crucial first step to success. But defining the game clearly isn't enough; your ELs have to be willing to get out into the game and start playing.

Stage 2: Getting Your EL in the Game

Your goal at this stage is to have the EL take ownership of the game or an objective—to ensure that the EL knows the goal is important and it's their responsibility to fulfill it. You'll know that has occurred when they start speaking about it and begin taking initiative. When your EL starts bringing up an assignment in meetings; when she puts update meetings on your agenda; when she starts bringing her own ideas to the issue—then she is demonstrating that she's engaged in the game. It's no longer just an idea under discussion.

Sometimes ELs are highly resistant to a given project—every boss has experienced this phenomenon. You might set out expectations and the EL might put the project off for an unspecified amount of time or overtly push back in a way that says, "I'm not committed to this."

The three main causes of push-back are:

1. Valid objections about timing, organizational hurdles, or competing priorities
2. An unconstructive EL/SL relationship

3. The EL's limited self-belief or limited ability to achieve the goal

Let's start by looking at the first cause of push-back: *valid concerns about timing, organizational hurdles, or competing priorities.* If the EL tells you "I just don't have the manpower to do this," no amount of cajoling or coaching in the world can help him create success. No matter how committed they might be, an EL without the resources or support structure to be effective is doomed to fail, and a commitment is really irrelevant.

I worked in one company where a particular Senior Leader continued to dump work on an EL—just dump, dump, dump, dump, dump. The EL was working his behind off . . . and dropping balls everywhere. The SL was a "Yes Man" who just kept saying "yes" to his boss and passing down all the "yeses" to his EL. He spread his resources so thin that it caused major issues in the company. The EL needed to use what I call "positive push-back"—the push-back that comes not from laziness or lack of interest, but from making intelligent choices about what's important, given the existing circumstances and resources. It can take guts for an EL to "tell the Emperor he has no clothes" with positive push-back, because she is risking her paycheck and job security by saying "no" to her SL. Positive push-back is an incredibly important experience for SLs; it provides an in-the-trenches reality check for the SL who's not as close to the work as the EL. In light of the boss/employee dynamic, positive push-back indicates one or both of the following:

1. You've got a leader on your hands in your EL.
2. You've created an environment where your reports can be straight with you in their communication (not an everyday occurrence).

On one hand, a good EL might force her SL to become a better leader. On the other hand, an EL won't accept coaching by anyone with whom she does not have a constructive relationship. As I've mentioned, this is the main reason why ELs walk out the door. It's not that they dislike the company; it's their relationship with their manager. This brings us to the second cause of push-back.

An unconstructive EL/SL relationship. Stephen R. Covey has often been quoted: "Relationship first, results second." Nowhere is this more important than in the EL/SL relationship. Indeed, the existing relationship itself can be a hurdle to creating the clear, honest, and empowering conversations that are necessary for success.

The EL/SL relationship can be likened to a marriage where couples have patterns of relating, some of which are less constructive than others. An unconstructive relationship between EL and SL is like a marriage that isn't working in some way. The couple spends their entire time arguing about the children. That's not a strategy for sorting out the relationship, of course. They must first see what in the relationship isn't working before they can focus meaningfully on external objectives. In other words, they need to shift the relationship, or they'll continue dancing the same way they have been dancing, and the resistance will continue. These dances are often ingrained and unintentional, but they're there nonetheless, and they lead to either overt or covert resistance to the SL by the EL (and vice versa).

Dynamics such as these are much more common than you might expect and can range from the subtle to the obvious. No matter what it looks like on the outside, an unconstructive EL/SL relationship will not get resolved by focusing on performance objectives. Any attempt the SL makes to "coach" an EL on the objectives in the context of a relationship like this has about as much chance of succeeding as a golf cart in a monster truck rally.

This can show up in the form of the SL saying, "Can you do this for me?" and the EL responding, "No, I can't do it." The SL can threaten, but the EL might threaten back, which is not very constructive on the part of either person.

Resistance can also show up when the SL is really excited about a particular project or initiative and the EL gets on board only halfheartedly. Another resistance pattern finds the SL saying things that cause anxiety or fuel the EL's fears; then the EL gets confused, overwhelmed, or paralyzed, and either cannot or will not move into action. For example, the SL might say, "I want you to present at the quarterly meeting. It's going to be very difficult and I'm not sure you can do it, but give it a try anyway." In this case, the SL is more than unsupportive—he's actually feeding the EL's fears and insecurities. In another resistance pattern, the SL brings up concerns and the EL tries to convince the SL that the concerns are not valid. In this situation, the EL won't look at herself, acknowledge the Senior Leader's input, or accept his point of view. The common denominator in all these resistance dances is the lack of clear performance expectations. Expectations exist in the context of a relationship. It's very difficult to set clear, meaningful expectations when the relationship isn't working.

For any issue to be resolved, someone must first take ownership of the issue. Clearly, when an SL is in charge of the team, it's ultimately his responsibility to acknowledge that an issue exists and to take ownership of that problem. Yes, it takes two to tango, but the boss leads.

A Simple Issue Resolution Model. Any time anyone is accused of anything, it's human nature to put up defences. Difficult conversations and the positions expressed in them are often interpreted as an attack. No real communication occurs when people are attacking or defending. Building a coaching relationship and resolving issues simply isn't going to happen when this type of behaviour is going on.

Here are the key steps to opening a dialogue that diffuses and resolves the issue before it escalates:

1. Take responsibility for the issue—it's my issue, not the other person's.
2. Check your intention. Is it really to resolve the issue, or are you hoping to prove that you were right or they were wrong? If it's the latter, don't bother even trying.
3. Ask for permission to speak about the issue. This can be a simple, "Joe, do you have a few minutes? I'd like to talk to you about X."
4. State the *facts* of the situation, free from your interpretations of what happened.
5. Ask what the facts mean or why they happened *instead* of stating your opinion about them as if it were the truth.
6. Continually loop back and check interpretation of new data as it emerges in the conversation.

Let's say the pattern in question is one in which the SL continually makes requests of the EL and the EL continually declines or doesn't take action on those requests. An SL might have an opinion about what that means, so the data hits the filter, which is made up of attitudes, assumptions, and beliefs. Perhaps the SL has a filter about ELs—maybe even about this EL in particular—that he's a slacker or doesn't care. That filter colours all data that's seen through it, *an interpretation of the data is formed that is not the same as the data itself*, and as in the diagram, the angle changes; the data becomes skewed by the refraction of the SL's filter (or perception). So if the filter is "he's a slacker and doesn't care," whatever data comes in will always be unconsciously skewed to fit that belief.

Filter of Interpretation

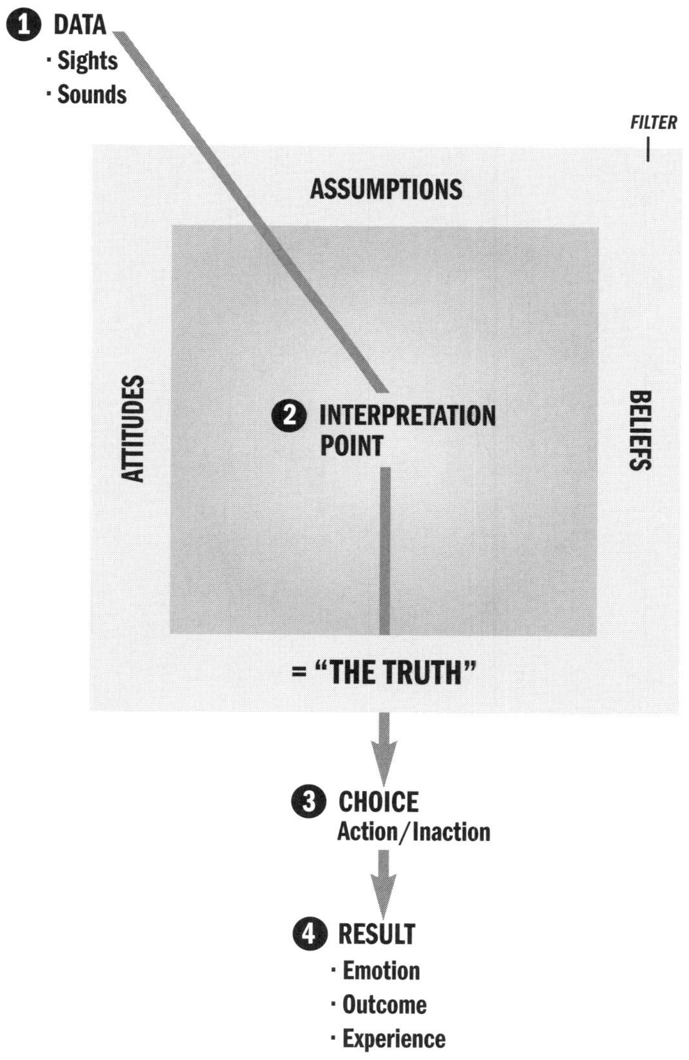

That elicits certain types of behaviour and results for the SL: being curt, impatient, frustrated, etc. And the dance continues.

When there are issues to be resolved in a relationship, people usually handle things in the opposite direction from which it occurred. Originally, 1: Data happened. 2: There was an interpretation. 3: There was a choice and action. 4: There was a result. When people try to resolve an issue by starting at Number 4—the result—they rarely get back to Number 1. They come in guns blazing, really frustrated or ticked off (or at minimum, quietly steaming). They think the other party isn't listening or doesn't care. Again, this is just as true in a marriage as it is in a relationship between an SL and an EL. Then they state their interpretation as if it's the truth. "I work really hard and you don't want to work the extra hours!" Now that's an interpretation stated as a truth, and it may well not be the case.

When the boss states his interpretation as the truth, the EL either puts up her defences or just appears to submit—but she's most likely seething on the inside. No one wins an argument this way. The boss might feel as though he's won, but he hasn't, because the EL is just planning her next withdrawal or attack. That's why I prefer Issue Resolution to Conflict Resolution. Usually, conflict is just a bunch of little, unresolved issues that build up until something small happens and suddenly, ka-boom! The Issue Resolution approach can be used to resolve small matters in a nanosecond so you don't have to wait until there's a big conflict or blow-up. Start from the top and state the data instead of coming from Number 4, the result.

Here's an example of the kind of approach that would be appropriate in a breakdown like this:

"I've got an issue that I want to talk about," (taking ownership) you might begin. "It's something that's not working. I want to have a conversation with you about it. Do you have a few minutes?" (asking for permission).

Acknowledge that there's an issue, as in: "I notice that whenever I make a request, you decline it. It often creates a situation where you yell and I yell back."

Stick with facts, not interpretations: "I've made two separate requests about getting started on the Anderson project, once in our biweekly meeting and once at lunch on Thursday (stating the data using specific date/time if possible). I still haven't seen the initial briefing document. Do you recall that?"

Once they recall, and/or agreement on the data is reached, as an SL, your next job is to check out those facts—"So what's going on? I don't understand why I haven't got the briefing yet."—or, alternately, then checking if your own SL interpretation is accurate: "I'm wondering if you've got concerns about moving forward..."

Asking a question, instead of stating an interpretation (which is loaded with assumptions, attitudes, and beliefs) as *the truth* gives the other person the opportunity to clarify what's really going on versus feeling he has to defend a perceived attack. Now a real conversation can take place, and the negative or resistant pattern can be broken. You can be constructive about what's missing or what needs to be put into the relationship.

As the SL, you're looking to shift the dance and get the conversation started. Only once a shift in the relationship is created by using Issue Resolution or some other means, can useful performance expectations for the EL be created.

That's how you change the dance.

Now let's look at the third cause of push-back: the EL's *limited self-belief or limited ability to achieve the goal.* Until now, we've been discussing issues that must be addressed or situations that must be overcome *before* you can shift into your coaching role. You can't be an effective coach if the EL/SL relationship isn't a constructive one. You also can't be an effective coach if your EL is resisting the project because of valid objections about timing, organizational hurdles, or competing priorities. By contrast, this next cause of push-back—an EL's limited skill or self-belief—isn't resistance to the request itself but reflects their doubts about fulfilling on it. Rather than being a hurdle you have to surmount before you can even begin supporting them, it likely indicates a precise need for some form of training or coaching.

Let's begin with the training need. It's usually easy to identify and solve the problem of a skill gap. If you've asked your EL to take on a particularly technical project, both of you will realize fairly quickly (sometimes even before the work is begun) if the EL simply doesn't have the necessary skill set. When you recognize this skill gap, fill it with training (or mentoring, as described earlier). You can certainly send the EL away to seminars, workshops, and classes where she can acquire the formal training necessary—or, when it's appropriate, you can do the training yourself. The basic training approach is simple although obviously the content can be quite complex. The approach applies in any setting, from training your EL at the office to teaching your child to tie his shoes. Here are the steps:

1. Show how the task is done.
2. Explain how the task is done.
3. Watch the trainees perform the task themselves.
4. Offer feedback.

For example, if you'd like an employee to begin logging numbers in a particular software program that he's never used before, you'll first sit down and log those numbers yourself as he watches.

Then you'll explain the process that you just went through, and maybe even write, draw, or chart it step by step. Next you'll ask the employee to log the numbers himself, and this time, you'll be the onlooker. Finally, you can go over and resolve any mistakes that the employee made or offer suggestions for shortcuts to use next time.

Training can be a relatively quick and painless way to address a clear skill-gap issue particularly technical skill-gap. Sometimes, however, you'll find that there is no obvious skill gap and that what you're dealing with is simply limited self-belief on the EL's part. If you find that the EL doesn't think he can do it, or expresses a lack of confidence, and you think he *is* capable—that's a great opportunity to move into Stage 3, coaching! So, read on. In the next chapter, we'll look at Core Coaching Principles, seven principles to instill in yourself and the EL you're coaching that will revolutionize the relationship and dramatically increase your ability to produce results.

12

Core Coaching Principles

In the previous chapter, we talked about some scenarios that Senior Leaders need to address *before* coaching can begin. Our goal in that chapter was to create an environment in which an SL can shift into a coaching role most effectively. Now, let's move on to the *here and now* of coaching. In this chapter, we'll talk about my Seven Core Coaching Principles: ways of thinking about business—and in fact, about life—that will jumpstart your attitude, creativity, and output as a Senior Leader. These principles are crucial for you to instill in the Emerging Leaders you coach and will help you understand what makes your ELs—or any employee—tick. They'll also give you some vocabulary for describing and analyzing your own experiences, which will enable you to shift into the coaching role with self-awareness and flexibility. We'll look at each of these Principles in detail:

1. The Principle of Motivation
2. The Principle of Forward Thinking
3. The Principle of Perspective
4. The Principle of Accountability
5. The Blind-Spot Principle
6. The Principle of Immediacy
7. The Principle of Authenticity

The Principle of Motivation

Let's be frank: all of us, whether we're aware of it or not, approach our tasks at work and at home with the attitude of, "What's in it for me?" This doesn't mean that we're operating from a selfish or negative standpoint; we simply have underlying desires that we hope to fulfill in our professional and personal lives and these shape the way we approach our things. Have you ever seen picketers on strike wearing sandwich boards with their union's slogan? Or, for that matter, a guy on the sidewalk wearing a sign advertising two-for-one subs at the deli? Consider that everyone around you is walking around the world with a sandwich board that broadcasts their message just as clearly as any picketer or sales rep: WIIFM—What's In It For Me?

But even if we all admit that we're walking around in WIIFM sandwich boards—that we're looking to get a return on each of our investments of money, time, focus, emotion, or anything else—we don't often disclose exactly *what kind* of return is important to us. I like to think of motivation as an iceberg. You've probably heard that only 10 percent of the ice is actually visible above the ocean's surface, while the other 90 percent is underwater, right? Well, I've found that the same holds true for a person's motivations. When you're working with ELs on a project, you've got a few clues that help you think about what's motivating them to succeed: their résumé, the way they behave (how quickly they get things done, whether or not they engage actively with the rest of the team), and the things they say to you and others. But that's only 10 percent of their story. To really engage with your ELs and get the most out of them, you've got to have a sense of what's below the water.

If you want to encourage a certain behaviour or outcome from an EL, if you want them to behave differently from what they've done in the past, you've got to find out how making a change would be in their best interest. What drives them? There are different motivators, but I've identified four that are most common, particularly in the workplace context. It's important to remember that we are usually driven by a combination of these, but in most cases there will be one or two that are primary drivers of behaviour in business.

Power or status. Some people are driven by a desire to obtain power. They have a strong need to control their own destiny and that of others in order to win at whatever game they are playing. We're used to thinking of this as a negative inclination, a desire to control or exploit. But it's a desire that also can be expressed very positively: the more power you have, the greater ability you have to accomplish your goals. For example, Hitler had an enormous need for power, but so did Mother Teresa. They, of course, met this need in diametrically opposed ways. People who are driven by power are passionate about winning, leading other people, achieving position, and building key relationships. All of these ultimately give them a greater ability to accomplish their goals. Overextensions of this motivator can lead individuals to seek power for power's sake. Also, people who are driven by power may be tempted to think of their own advancement as more important than the needs of others. To communicate effectively with these ELs, you'll want to focus on opportunities for them to lead, allude subtly to how their positions will be advanced, and emphasize how their positions and power can be used to help the cause.

Learning, exploration, and understanding. These ELs are very objective, rational people who are driven by curiosity and who want to understand the world, solve problems, and figure out how things work. They value intellectual processes highly. ELs who are motivated by a desire to learn are often reluctant to stay in any one position for very long, because once they've absorbed all that's new, they fear stagnation. If they *do* enjoy the stability of a longer-term role, it must be one that allows for continued learning. Their restlessness isn't necessarily a character flaw; they just need regular opportunities to tackle fresh challenges and/or projects that break new ground and challenge them intellectually. They'll die on the vine if they're put into roles that require more maintenance and less innovation. Is there a way to create opportunities for them to learn and innovate and at the same time honour the business's priorities? Overextended, this driver can lead to their quest for knowledge and understanding overwhelming other practical areas of their lives, such as family or finances. Their interest in learning new things can have them moving on prematurely to new roles or projects. To communicate powerfully with these ELs, focus on objective data, rational experience, and solving problems. Present well-thought-out research with your conclusions.

Money or utility. If money is what makes your ELs tick, they are the kind of people who are passionate about capitalism. They're interested in and extremely good at creatively applying resources like time, money, and energy to get the maximum return, financial or otherwise. These ELs are extremely practical people who value efficiency and will have a common bias toward asking, "What's the bottom line?" They will become frustrated and annoyed in the face of inappropriately applied resources and are also highly aware of their own earning power. They are sensitive to their compensation and pay scales and will likely keep score cards of their income versus that of others in the company and similar companies. If they feel that they aren't being fairly financially rewarded or earning the money they deserve, expect to hear about it. To communicate with these ELs, focus on the ROI, prove where the return on investment of resources and time will occur, and make sure the ROI discussed is of interest to them.

Developing others. You might find yourself with the opportunity to coach ELs who are naturally attuned to other people. They are the coaches of the future. They either do, or will, value spending time with their own reports, helping them meet objectives and maximize their potential. They enjoy helping their team tackle problems they struggle with and having career development conversations; they have a finger on the pulse of the human elements of their team, your organization, and your customers. They love worthy causes. Their first question about any project will be: "What is the impact on the people involved?" When this motivator is overextended, there might be a tendency to put themselves or the business results last and to create lose/win relationships where their employees take advantage of them. To communicate powerfully with these people, focus on the human element and how people will benefit. Emphasize how conflict could be diminished or the potential of the people involved will be increased.

These four motivators—power, learning, money, and developing others—are the common pillars of motivation for you to be on the lookout for with your ELs as you begin coaching them. Indeed, since it's overwhelmingly typical that we are good at what we enjoy, these motivators will point to the work your ELs will do well. Your coaching will be exponentially more effective if you can approach an EL with an understanding of *why* he comes into the office every morning. If you begin framing ideas and projects in terms of how he can maximize his return in whatever area he values most, new doors will open for both of you.

So how do you find these underlying motivators? It's a conversation you can begin to have even in the hiring stage: "Why are you interested in this position in particular? What did you like most about your last role? What do you hope to gain?" Of course, motivators don't always reveal themselves in a naked fashion. A candidate (whether coming from the outside or transferring from within) is not likely to say, "I want this position because of the money." However, if you explore things such as what they do for fun, their prized possession, or a moment in their life that has meant the most to them, you'll find clues to motivation within their responses.

But perhaps your EL is someone who's been on your team for awhile, someone you inherited from another department. In that situation, his or her motivators can also become evident through the work-history interviews described in chapter 7. They may also come to light of their own accord, simply because you have become aware of what they are. For example, now that you know that learning is a motivator, you might notice much more readily that Sue loves spending time researching documents and planning strategy, and now it will be clear to you *why*. Or when you see that Joe is always out supporting his team, that observation will flip on the "developing others" lightbulb in your mind.

The good news is that if, as we discussed in chapter 10, you are able to clearly delineate between your duties as manager and your offerings as coach, then you are helping build the foundation for partnership with your EL. With partnership as the context for your relationship, these motivators will often make themselves evident simply through your opened channels of communication and increased awareness that they exist in the first place.

Finally, with the right assessment tools, you can get extremely insightful, practical, and valuable information about what motivates your employees—and how best to manage them using that information. A reliable ten-minute online assessment tool, like the ones we use in our programs, can give you a clear portrait of an EL's motivators and prepare you to move forward with the best outcome for both of you in mind.

The Principle of Forward Thinking

A few years ago, I started getting seriously involved in cycling. A cyclist friend of mine was impressed enough with my training to say, "You know, you should really think about doing a twenty-four-hour mountain bike race in the solo category." The first time he mentioned it, I thought it was a crazy idea—something only daredevils and hardcore athletes would do. But slowly, the idea started to grow on me, until finally, one January, I bit the bullet and signed up for a twenty-four-hour solo race that would take place the following August.

Suddenly, my whole attitude and approach toward cycling was transformed: I started working with a coach, I hired a mechanic to professionally maintain my bike, I changed my diet, and I intensified my training. I was petrified and unbelievably excited at the same time. I ultimately completed the race in August, but when did the race really begin for me? In January, when I signed up. By declaring and committing to a future for myself, I had made that future my reality *in the present.* I began behaving like a twenty-four-hour soloist in January, even though I wouldn't actually be one until August.

This is what I mean by the Principle of Forward Thinking: the ability to create futures for ourselves that impact us *now* in the present. The fascinating thing is that this is one of the most underestimated but enormously impacting tools that SLs can use when coaching and managing their ELs. It's actually uncannily simple to create a future for your EL to grow into that engages them and also fully leverages their talents now. It's because of this principle that the "Become a co-creator of the EL's future" practice is the first practice discussed in chapter 8, "Create Partnership." And it's also why the development plans in chapter 9 are so important. Find tangible ways to link your ELs' aspirations with their current skills and career steps, and you'll be leaps and bounds beyond your competition in engaging and keeping them. If you create the context, if you really start the wheels turning in the ELs' minds, their futures will create themselves.

Here's another example: I coached an EL who was working in professional services. He wanted to become a partner in his firm, but the existing partners weren't particularly interested in adding more partners. My client was beginning to seriously consider looking elsewhere or striking out on his own. So the two of us sat down and created a future that lit him up. "You're going to be partner in two years." The partners in the firm had no idea that that was the model we were operating under, but my client began to change his behaviour. He started having completely different conversations; he started taking greater ownership, making bigger decisions, taking more initiative, and becoming far more assertive; he started *acting like a partner*. The partners noticed—how could they not? And within eighteen months, *he was a partner*. It's that simple; it's that powerful.

In summary, the Principle of Forward Thinking determines that it's the future we create (consciously or unconsciously) that gives us who we are in any moment. Whether it's being relaxed on Friday because you're looking forward to the weekend, being focused because you signed up for the twenty-four-hour race, or being a leader because you declared that you'll be a partner in two years, *it's the context you create for your future that gives you who you're being and how you act in the present.* Clearly then, it follows that actively creating a compelling future *has value now*.

Conversely, the Principle of Forward Thinking can have a dramatically negative effect for SLs and ELs alike if it's left untended, particularly when you're just accepting that things are "okay." You see, without actively creating what the future looks like, it's human nature to default to what's already there—more of the same scenario, or perhaps only slightly better. That "default" future is likely nowhere near as compelling when compared to what could be possible if the future were actively discussed and created. We as people will naturally create futures as we always have, but the ones we *consciously* cultivate will be far more compelling and powerful to us. That's why it's so critical to leverage this principle. Your EL will be engaged and energized because he's excited about his future prospects, and you'll start receiving the value of his future level of performance now—not later, when the role is formally given. Not only will you have an employee performing at a higher level, but you'll also have an Emerging Leader who's more dedicated and invested than he might be otherwise. The future contexts are disarmingly easy to create and they start having a real, measurable impact right away.

The Principle of Perspective

We've all heard the expression, "I'll believe it when I see it." But Wayne Dyer is right when he says the inverse is more true: you'll see it when you believe it. As people, we continually create realities for ourselves based on the attitudes and beliefs that we hold, whether they're conscious or not. You've probably had the common experience of walking outside wearing your sunglasses on a beautiful, sunny day. At some point, you remember you're wearing your sunglasses, and the moment you take them off, you're surprised to see—"Holy cow, it's so bright out here!" These sunglasses are a great analogy for the many filters that we, as human beings, wear all the time but have forgotten about. For example, you probably didn't wake up this morning and say to yourself, "Today, I will look at the world like a woman (or man)!" But whether you thought about it or not, that filter has a clear and meaningful impact not only on how you looked at the world all day but *what you actually saw during the day.*

We have countless other filters. Once you become a parent, you start noticing kids everywhere; you start thinking about schools and daycare and college savings programs. If you're in a particular industry, you'll read the financial section of the paper with an eye for anything that affects that industry. When you buy a new car, you'll start noticing the same make and model and color everywhere you go. They've been there all along, but suddenly you have a filter for them, and you become conscious of them. Neurologists call this phenomenon *reticular activation*. We're bombarded by millions of bits of sensory information per second; there's no way for our conscious minds to process them all with the same weight. So our reticular activator, essentially the gateway to our conscious awareness, uses these filters to select and separate those things that might have particular meaning to us from the rest of the stimuli that's irrelevant or superfluous.

We need our reticular activator to avoid going crazy from overload. But sometimes, our filters can distort reality and work against us. Our sunglasses protect our eyes from the glare of the sun, but they also keep us from seeing just how bright the world is. By the same token, once we start viewing our experiences through a particular filter, what we see is coloured by that filter and no longer accurately reflects reality. In other words, we begin to attach meaning or opinion to those experiences that might not have anything to do with the facts at hand.

Here's an example. Let's say you've been invited to give a presentation in front of the Board of Directors of your organization. You walk into the room and say hello, and everyone at the conference table just stares at their laptops. You set up your presentation and go through it, and still everyone stares at their laptops without saying anything, giving you no feedback whatsoever. When you leave that boardroom, there's any number of conclusions you could draw. You might think it went terribly, or the Board has no respect for your work, or they're a bunch of arrogant jerks, or they were all having a bad day, or you're too young and have no credibility, or you're just a brutal presenter. All of these ideas are interpretations of the actual experience, which was, simply: you went in, gave your presentation, no one said anything, and you left.

Every different person coming out of that experience would have a different interpretation of it, based on their own filters. But here's the catch: our interpretation becomes a filter that then impacts the *next* experience for you and others. If you decide, for example, that no one said anything in the boardroom because you're a brutal presenter, the next time you're asked to present, you might decline the opportunity. If you decline a future opportunity or two to present, people may notice this and make their own interpretation ("that person lacks confidence," perhaps). Then they will respond accordingly to your new behaviour (by not asking you to present again, perhaps), and you'll then respond to *their* response (possibly by no longer bringing ideas forward). This cycle is addictive, and can spiral downwards over time. Like making a photocopy of a photocopy of a photocopy, everyone's making interpretations of interpretations of interpretations, and pretty soon everyone is so far removed from the initial facts that it's impossible to ever know what set off the negative cycle. Each experience can colour the next in turn.

In the coaching realm, SLs will save themselves a lot of grief if they recognize that, in our daily lives, people are rarely objective. Indeed, an incredibly pervasive problem for all of us is that *we will often make the perceived facts of an experience and our interpretation of the experience one and the same*. To coach effectively, you need to become acutely aware of the difference between the EL's opinion of what happened and what actually happened. And you also need to be aware of your own filters, because you might be operating based on opinion rather than fact too. There's a Peanuts cartoon where Charlie Brown draws a picture of a man with his hands behind his back, and he shows it to Linus. Linus says, "Charlie Brown, I know why you drew that man with his hands behind his back. You're demonstrating that he feels insecure about the world we live in." And Charlie Brown says, "No, I just don't know how to draw hands." When your ELs come to you with an opinion about Charlie Brown's drawing, bring them back to looking at the drawing itself. Remind them that it's natural to create interpretations about what happened and to add meaning to those events, but those stories are not necessarily the truth, and questioning those interpretations is critical. That's how you break the cycle of interpretation addiction.

The Principle of Accountability

I've developed the Principle of Accountability from my own coaching experience and from the very important work of others, like Neale Donald Walsh in *Conversations with God* and Thomas Leonard (the father of the modern coaching movement and founder of Coach U, where I received my coach training) in *The Portable Coach*, and from the ideas of the Landmark Forum and Constellation Learning, among others. The Principle of Accountability is actually a type of filter, a way of looking at the world. It is a bedrock principle without which we sell out on our tremendous capacity to effect change and produce results. Simply defined, the Principle of Accountability invites us to own the following statement: "I am causing *all* of the results in my life."

Our greatest leverage point for creating change is not changing what's around us; it's changing ourselves. When we finger-point at an outside factor—some external circumstance or person—as the source of an undesirable result in our lives, where does the power lie? With that outside factor, of course. If we say, "My business isn't growing because the economy is stagnating," all the power to grow the business lies with the economy. By the same token, if an EL is waiting for management to provide the perfect opportunity for her to advance her career, the power lies with the organization . . . and, odds are, her career will be on hold for a long time.

You might be thinking, "Okay, but if these people didn't take ownership of their business or career success, clearly they're not being responsible." Let's take it a step further.

Now notice I didn't ask you to accept the statement, "I am causing *most* of the results in my life." In truth, I'm suggesting that you're causing *all* of them. When I first have a conversation with clients about the Principle of Accountability, I introduce the principle to them, and most of the time, they say, "Yeah, that makes a lot of sense, I already believe that!" But then I ask them, "So, what about the state the economy is in? What about the person who broke into your car? Or the fact that when you went on your ski holiday there wasn't enough snow? Did you cause those results?" And their response is, "Well, of course not! I didn't book my ski trip to go golfing or ask for my car to be burglarized."

If whether you caused those results is debatable, why don't I ask people to accept accountability for 97 percent of the results in their life and put those results "clearly" not caused by them in the remaining 3 percent? Well, because then there's an out. It allows you to slowly start jamming everything that doesn't suit you into the "debatable 3 percent" that you're not responsible for. On some level you could argue that the state of the global economy legitimately resides in the debatable 3 percent. But what about the fact that your boss is a poor manager—where does that lie? Or what about the fact that there is a freeze on promotions and few opportunities for advancement in your company? It's tempting, easy, and likely that they will all slide into the 3 percent of convenience, where the slippery slope of abdicating responsibility begins. So I invite my clients to consider that they are accountable for 100 percent of the results in their lives. In actuality, you *are* responsible for your position in the global economy, and you *do* have an impact on how your boss manages you. In adopting this principle, you own it all, and the back door disappears.

If you adopt the position that you have created all of the results in your life, there are two major implications. First, it's a bit scary. After all, you're now the one who's created all those results you're less than proud of—not always an easy pill to swallow. Second, however, it's entirely empowering. If I've created the reality that I haven't moved ahead in my career, then I can create a different reality, too. I can create a solution. This is *not* about placing blame or fault on yourself—goodness knows, there's enough of that to go around. If a project collapses, your response isn't to say, "I'm accountable; I shoulda/coulda/woulda . . ." Instead, accountability is a filter, a place to stand and look from. From this new vantage point, the same circumstances look entirely different. Accountability gently invites us to ask, "What did I do to cause that outcome?" It allows us to see opportunities to do something about negative outcomes as opposed to waiting for some circumstance or individual to change those outcomes for us. It shifts us from being a victim of a situation to being empowered and the cause of a different result.

So, as an SL, the Principle of Accountability is something you can propose to your ELs as a filter, as a way of looking at the world.

Throw it out for conversation, and ask them where they don't accept it and where they believe it's true. Have the conversation with them about the 3 percent of convenience. Don't suggest that they accept this principle as The Truth—it's not. But rather, suggest that they try it on as a filter. Things start getting interesting when we begin to take full accountability for all the choices we make and the results they produce in our lives. You'll find that it's a very effective distinction for both you and your EL to operate from in coaching conversations.

The Blind-Spot Principle

The research psychologists Joseph Luft and Harry Ingham developed a model of interpersonal behaviour called the Johari Window in 1955. It is very useful in framing two essential elements for increasing both your and your EL's effectiveness as leaders: vulnerability and feedback.

Johari Window

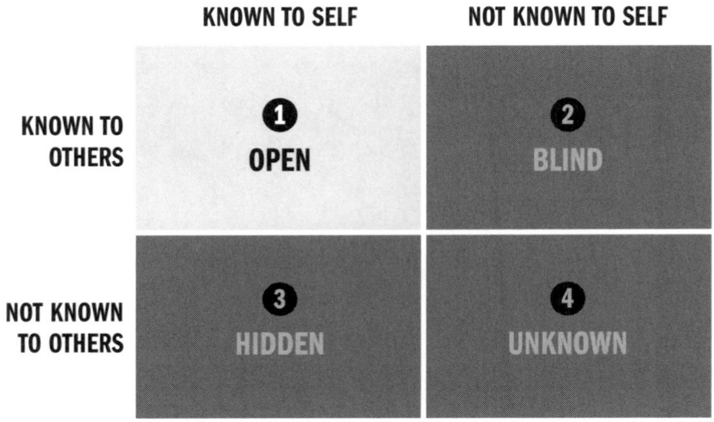

Quadrant 1: The areas of self-expression and power and openness refer to behaviour and motivation known by self and others.

Quadrant 2: These are our blind spots, where others can see things in us that we don't recognize.

Quadrant 3: This area is avoided or kept hidden and is characterized by what we know, but do not reveal to others.

Quadrant 4: This area points to behaviour and motivations that are not yet known by self or others.

We all have the most power and freedom to create results when we're operating in Quadrant 1, the open quadrant. Here, we have a clear understanding of ourselves, our motives, and our behaviours, and others do as well. There's nothing to hide and we're not blind to anything getting in our way. It's a powerful place to be. If we increase the size of this quadrant, it increases the potential we have to enact change and produce results. But how might you do that?

1. Share more with others (and thus move the lower border of the quadrant downward). It's in the hiding and concealing of things that we diminish our ability to act powerfully and to influence others. We've all tried operating with a secret—it's a difficult, awkward, and ultimately an ineffective approach to take. I'm not suggesting we share everything with everyone; that would hardly be appropriate. However, I've yet to meet an executive that's as open as either they'd like to be or need to be to produce the results they're committed to. More on this in the final principle, The Principle of Authenticity.

2. Be insatiably curious about yourself (and thus move the right hand border of the quadrant further to the right). When you adopt the Principle of Accountability discussed earlier, you are continually inquiring about your contribution to the situation as opposed to misplacing your attention elsewhere. The

accountability principle naturally encourages a practice of self-inquiry, and when self-inquiry is combined with requests for honest, genuine feedback from others, personal insight is the inevitable outcome. As more and more information that was previously unknown to me becomes known, the centre vertical line can quickly and dramatically move to the right as a result. Therefore, I'm acting in a more informed manner and the open quadrant expands.

Johari Window

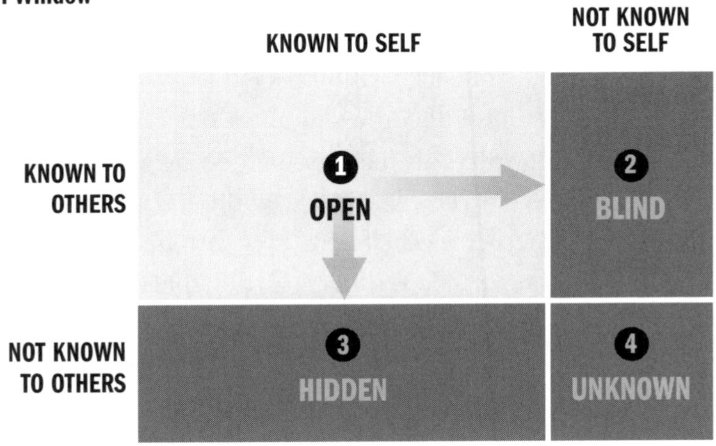

Now let's look at Quadrant 2 of the Johari Window in detail: things that are known to others, but—for whatever reason—unknown to us. Often, it's very easy to see another person's problems or flaws, but much more difficult to identify these things in ourselves. And at the same time that we're busy pinpointing other people's problems, they're doing the same to us and noticing things that we aren't aware of. This information is what I call our *blind spots*. Blind spots are a veritable orchard of low-hanging fruit when it comes to coaching. If we can begin to open each other's eyes to blind spots, we've found a very simple way of changing our behaviour and creating entirely different results.

The fact is that the axes in the Johari Window are all entirely flexible. By soliciting feedback from others, people invariably receive information that's in Quadrant 2. As that information is shared more and more that was previously known to others but unknown to me becomes known to all of us—it's no longer in my blind spot and becomes known to me where I can act on it. As a result, the line between Quadrants 1 and 2 shifts to the right, reflecting my greater capacity of freedom and power.

Let's look at a potentially familiar example: the film *The Truman Show*, which is an excellent metaphor for our blind spots. In the movie, Jim Carey plays Truman, an unknowing soul literally born into a carefully-constructed, artificial world. In fact, he's the product of a grand experiment created by a visionary TV producer. Everyone in Truman's life is actually an actor: his parents, friends, coworkers, people on the street—everyone. For thirty years, Truman has lived on the biggest stage set ever created. Truman's life is carefully orchestrated, meticulously captured on film, and transmitted to an eagerly awaiting outside world 24/7. Of course, Truman thinks his whole life is real; he doesn't know anything else. But slowly, over the course of the movie, clues about the real nature of his world start appearing. He starts to question more and more of what he took for granted until, ultimately, in the final scene of the movie, he stumbles upon a real exit door on the set of his world as he knows it. He faces the choice of leaving his artificial world or staying within it. For the first time, the producer's voice comes over a loudspeaker in Truman's world. The producer, who has grown to love Truman much as a parent would, implores him to stay: "You're afraid and that's why you can't leave. I've been with you throughout all your great experiences. You can't leave; you belong here with me." And Truman makes his choice.

While it's obvious that the TV producer created Truman's physical world, there's much more to his experience than the stage set. His world is also comprised of his hopes, dreams, aspirations, fears—and the list goes on. Truman created his own psychological artificial world based on the material artificial world around him.

Here's the rub: We're no different from Truman. We all create our own worlds on a regular basis (Johari Quadrants 1 and 3). We don't need visionary producers to construct realities for us; we're quite capable of creating our own fantasy lands, thank you very much. In fact, we live in them everyday. They're founded on assumptions, attitudes, and beliefs about the world we live in. Those worlds we create and our experiences of them shape what we desire, what we think we're capable of, and ultimately, the leaders we become in life.

It's inside your world of Quadrant 1 that you feel most at home. You've proven you can produce results there, but of course, your results are innately limited by what you're aware of. If you really want to expand the capabilities of your ELs as leaders, supporting them in identifying their blind spots through coaching and feedback is a tremendous gift that pays dividends again and again.

Emerging Leaders, by definition, are beginning to demonstrate their leadership competence and potential. But like all of us, they have blind spots in their growing leadership. What follows is a list of common behavioural blind spots of Emerging Leaders. Don't be put off by the list as a whole—you'd be hard pressed to find any employee who has all of these blind spots. These are just individual behaviours to look for in your coaching that might be holding an EL back.

A Sampling of Common EL Behavioural Blind-Spots

Over-relying on previous skill sets. Defaulting to the technical competence of their previous roles and not focusing on their growing strategic responsibilities; getting stuck in the weeds.

Not taking full ownership. Avoiding responsibility for a result or a situation, or blaming others or circumstance.

Relying solely on logic to motivate or influence others, or the opposite, **relying mostly on emotion** to motivate or enrol others.

Treating previous peers as "buddies" after promotion. Relating to their staff as they did before they were promoted without acknowledging the new boss/employee relationship.

Demanding compliance vs. enrolling their team. Seeing only their own perspective and failing to stand in anyone else's shoes.

Claiming infallibility. Wanting to project a "have-it-all-together" image; refusing to acknowledge personal errors; not being open to contrary opinion and feedback.

Having a smaller, more limited organizational perspective. Not thinking beyond the current role to their boss' role (or their boss' boss' role) or the role of other stakeholders across the organization.

Withholding information. Keeping information to themselves so they can feel secure or in control of a situation.

Seeking recognition. Consistently and inappropriately seeking attention from SLs; taking credit where it isn't due or failing to share credit appropriately.

Being culturally inattentive. Lacking awareness about organizational culture and how things get accomplished in that culture.

Displaying promotion attachment. "Needing" a promotion as acknowledgement of their capabilities and the immediate next step in growing their career; discounting lateral opportunities or becoming frustrated when promotions simply aren't available.

Getting caught up in busy-ness or the firefighter mode. Reacting only to the "urgent" work; not lifting their head to tackle the work that really matters.

Succumbing to fraud syndrome. Despite demonstrated successes, continually questioning or downplaying their capability; resisting challenging opportunities that may provide career advancement.

Being critical and negative. Not giving new ideas fair consideration or consistently providing their opinion when it's not asked for.

Consistently interrupting others. This behaviour says, "What I have to say is more important than what you have to say." It can be unbelievably annoying for all involved.

Helicopter managing. Constantly hovering over their individual team members to make sure things are done properly or on time.

Lacking customer focus. Not managing or designing their departments to most effectively serve their customers (internal or external).

Managing by avoidance. Not making the tough decisions or dealing with sticky situations where conflict may occur.

Getting frozen by a negative past experience. They were on a promising trajectory until they were derailed by "that" event. They don't engage or demonstrate initiative the way they used to.

The Principle of Immediacy

This next Principle is an important complement to the Blind-spot Principle. It's a valuable method of helping people see their blind spots in a meaningful way. Immediacy means that you notice a particular experience between you and your EL here and now, in your current conversation. When you see this connection and share your experience with the EL in the moment, it immediately shifts the conversation from a "theoretical, out-there" understanding into a "visceral, now-I-see-it" understanding *in the moment* which is crucial for people to really "get" the impact versus just understand it theoretically. As an SL, you put yourself smack-dab in the middle, with the EL, of the experience he's been referring to. From here, the experience you have and your reactions to it provide an extremely meaningful basis from which to support your EL.

To increase your ability to use The Principle of Immediacy in your coaching conversations, here's an overview of the approach:

1. Look for parallel experiences between what the EL is doing with you and what they are describing as having happened in their world.
2. Share your experience of the EL directly with the EL in the moment.
3. Connect your experience to what they may be doing elsewhere in their world.

You might be familiar with the standard communication model that the words we use comprise approximately 10 percent of the message we're projecting. About 60 percent of that message is in our body language, and 30 percent is in our tone. So, 90 percent—or sometimes more—of what we're communicating is found outside of what we're saying. Communication, then, is not just the words expressed but also your experience of the EL's "being" a particular way. This can show up in countless forms, from calmness to frustration to anxiety to scattered thoughts, etc.

If you're coaching an EL and she's telling you, "I've had numerous conversations with Jerald and Sam and they just don't seem to be getting on board with the direction I've set," *look for parallel experiences* in which that happens in your conversation with the EL. We often behave consistently in various contexts, including the conversation the EL is having with you right in this moment.

In your conversation with the EL, when you find your mind wandering or hear your little voice commenting on the conversation ("I don't seem to be following where she's going right now. What's the point of what she's sharing? I don't get it."), you are actually inside the problem and are missing the opportunity. However, when you notice how your mind is chattering away about your experience and then ask, "I wonder if other people get lost in conversations with her the way I am right now? Do other people have difficulty seeing what the point is, too?"—you'll more effectively link how the EL's behaviour shows up in real life, "out there," versus the way she is describing it to you.

After you have noticed your experience and your reaction to it, you can move on to the final two steps: *sharing your "here and now" experience of the EL* and *connecting it with her world*. It might sound something like this: "I'm not sure where our conversation is going right now. You talk about one aspect of your situation with Jerald and Sam and then jump to another. I'm having difficulty understanding what you want and you seem scattered. I'm wondering if Jerald and Sam might be having a similar experience." You aren't saying she *is* that way; you're just saying that's the *experience* you're having in your exchange with her right now and making the links. Mirroring back your experience of the EL in the moment it happens provides a visceral understanding of their role in causing the situation and the message she might have projected in that situation and others like it.

This is a marked shift from the typical boss/employee dynamic. As an SL, you're used to hearing the problem simply as it's presented in an individual's words, and then offering a solution based on that. But any solution an SL offers, though quick and convenient, doesn't reveal the blind spot that caused the behaviour to begin with, and doesn't enable the EL to take responsibility for what really caused the situation.

The Principle of Authenticity

Anyone who's human suffers from being inauthentic on occasion, where we pretend certain things about ourselves to others. Sometimes—as in the example that follows—it can be overt, but often it's far more subtle. The impact, however, is universal: a diminished capacity to act powerfully in the situation. The Principle of Authenticity is a key tool for re-establishing your capacity to act.

Here's an embarrassing example from my life. A few years ago, I laid out a schedule of evenings I was going to go help out at an organization I volunteer with. I had committed to the evening of September 13th, but as the date approached, my work started to get crazy. I knew it was going to be a challenge to make the event. "I should call and cancel," I thought to myself three or four days before. But I was optimistic; I had made a commitment, and I decided to try to make it work somehow. On the evening of the 13th, however, I was completely swamped, and I knew it just wasn't going to happen. The last time I attended, I was one of more than fifty volunteers, and I did very basic work for them, so I justified to myself that anyone could do that work—they probably wouldn't even miss me. I skipped the appointment and worked late.

The following day, I got a voicemail from Grace, one of the organizers. "Hi, Jamie, just checking in. We were expecting you last night, and I just wanted to see if there was a breakdown on our end. Give me a quick buzz when you get a second." Oh no. I sat there strategizing. How could I get out of this without looking like a total moron? I started dialling the number, but then hung up. My mind raced. "What if I say ...?" I wanted to have all my angles covered; I worked through various counter-scenarios. Finally, filled with dread, I dialled the number.

"Hey, Grace, thanks for you call. Not sure what happened last night..." Lie #1.

"Was it on your calendar as the 13th?"

"Uhm. Let's see. I have October 4th and 13th, November 20th . . ." Lie #2. Note my clever avoidance of the September 13th date.

"Okay, Jamie, let me just get Evan in here so we can sort this out," Grace said. I was digging the hole deeper. Evan was the event coordinator with whom I'd planned my schedule. I knew I definitely had been on his list for last night.

Grace got back on the phone with Evan. "For Evan's benefit, Jamie, you didn't have it in your calendar, did you?"

I felt like a boxer, bobbing and weaving, avoiding the question. Finally, I mumbled, "No, I didn't have it in my calendar." Lie #3.

"Okay, Jamie, sorry to waste your time. I need to have a conversation with Evan."

How did I get myself into this? I was completely embarrassed about my assumption of not even being missed at the event, and by the despicable and uncharacteristic things I'd said to cover it up. I could not believe what I'd just done. Now Evan would have to deal with my screw-up and lies. Time stopped; my hands got clammy. A voice in my head screamed, "For goodness sake, tell the truth!"

"Wait, Grace. Evan. I'm utterly embarrassed to say this, but I lied. I was completely overwhelmed with my commitments this week. I didn't realize you were counting on me, and frankly, I didn't think I'd be missed."

"Jamie, thank you for being honest."

Just like the proverb says: "The truth shall set you free." I was embarrassed and relieved, but most importantly, I didn't have to pretend anymore. The matter got cleared up right then and there—done and dusted.

The value of dealing with what we're hiding from others cannot be overstated. By being straight with others, not only does the issue get resolved, but the relationship has a clean slate again. My example is intended to be a small and seemingly "unimportant" one, yet unaddressed, it would potentially have led to greater lies and/or less and less ability to deal powerfully with the situation. All big lies started at some point as little lies. Contrast my example with the recent arrest of Wall Street legend Bernard Madoff for what will probably go down as the greatest swindle in Wall Street history—the defrauding of investors of a staggering $50 billion in a carefully constructed Ponzi scheme. The official FBI criminal complaint document states that when two federal agents arrived at Mr. Madoff's apartment, he told them, "There is no innocent explanation." The agents say that he told them "he paid investors with money that wasn't there," that he was "broke" and that he expected to go to jail. Shortly thereafter, the *New York Times* reported on his first public admission of guilt at a federal courtroom hearing. He said, "I knew what I was doing was wrong, indeed criminal. When I began the Ponzi scheme, I believed it would end shortly, and I would be able to extricate myself and my clients." But getting out of the entanglement "proved difficult, and ultimately impossible.

As the years went by, I realized this day, and my arrest, would inevitably come."[8]

While Bernard Madoff will spend a lot of time in jail, his realization that his arrest was inevitable shows that he hasn't been free for years—he was jailed by his thoughts of being found out. This is clearly a dramatic example, but it points to the lack of freedom that even the world's smartest and seemingly most powerful people experience when they hide the truth.

Most of us are more inauthentic than we'd care to admit. While outright, verbalized lies—like the embarrassing one I told or the grandiose ones of Mr. Madoff—are obvious to us even as we tell them, there are more insidious mistruths that we constantly create that are part of being human. We pretend one thing while something else is true for us. Whenever we're hiding something, we create a lack of freedom and limit our ability to produce results. In the situation with Grace and Evan, I was strategizing, trying to figure out how to get out of it, get around it, say the right thing, and look good. I was doing a fancy dance in the conversation to avoid what was really going on.

The Principle of Authenticity teaches us that when we own up to what we've been hiding—when we get authentic—we're free again. Sure, there may be consequences we'll need to deal with in the short term, but we gain the freedom to deal with the situation and find solutions. All the energy spent on maintaining the façade is no longer needed and we can move forward with power again.

Apologizing is one way of being authentic. "I'm sorry, I screwed up." Or, "I'm sorry, I don't know how to do that. I've never tried that before. I don't have a ready answer." These are phrases that, frankly, we rarely hear in the business world, or maybe even in

8. Henriques, Diana B. and Jack Healy. 2009. "Madoff Goes to Jail After Guilty Pleas." *New York Times*, March 12.

the world in general. We all want to look good and avoid mistakes. But the fact is that when we do hear someone owning up to what's really true for them, even if it's an imperfection, it's incredibly disarming, because it's not common practice. Being authentic can also require us to be vulnerable. The root of the word *vulnerability* is the Latin word *vulnus*, which means *wound*. Being vulnerable literally means to show others that you are woundable—that you are human. It's very compelling, because it speaks to the humanity in all of us and gives others permission to be open and honest as well. We spend a lot of time walking around pretending to be bulletproof. The problem is that if the bullets can't get in, neither can contributions, genuine communication, connectedness, and support.

I invite you to try authenticity on for size. Indeed the best way to encourage it in your team is to model it yourself. When you face the real issue, you'll find that dramatically different possibilities will open up for you.

Those are the Seven Core Coaching Principles. Each is a way of looking at the world and approaching situations with others that, if you take them to heart, can break down barriers and open up possibilities for results, both in your own work and in the work you do with ELs. But these are all broad-brush sweeps. In the next chapter, we'll return to the coaching easel with a fine brush and fill in the details. Now that you have an understanding of the coaching environment and the core distinctions that will help you and your ELs succeed, let's look at the coaching process and the day-to-day activities and approaches you can take on when working with ELs.

13

The Good-Enough Coach: A Simple Coaching Model

In chapter 11, we discussed Stages 1 and 2 of my coaching model, *defining the game* and *getting ELs engaged in the game*, both of which must be completed before coaching can begin. In chapter 12, I talked about seven core coaching principles that will help ground you in some fundamental coaching principles. So now we can actually deal with Stage 3, the coaching process itself.

Before we begin, however, let's ease off the accelerator for a moment. If you're anything like the majority of SLs, you might think that coaching ELs sounds like a great idea in theory, but you've got reservations about it in practice. In my experience, Senior Leaders are hesitant about coaching for two reasons:

1. They're so busy with the daily demands of running the business that they don't have time to devote to coaching; or
2. They simply don't have the inclination or interest to develop their ELs and make coaching a priority.

These are both perfectly valid reasons to hesitate. The reality is, however, that developing the leaders of tomorrow is absolutely crucial to the success of your enterprise, and coaching is proven to be one of the most effective leadership development tools. Any Senior Leader wants to be at the head of a team that can manage itself—that can get the work done without constant oversight and babysitting, but at the same time can be relied on to do the job well. The bottom line in any organization is to save time and energy and still produce the quality results that have earned your organization the reputation it enjoys today. One of the best ways to achieve this ethic among your Emerging Leaders—and to have it stick—is through coaching. It all comes down to the old adage: Give a man a fish, and he'll eat for one day. Teach him to fish, and he'll eat for a lifetime. Yes, teaching your ELs to fish will cost you a little time upfront, but in the long run, you'll have created independence and leadership, an immeasurable return on your investment.

The good news is that your time investment doesn't have to be as hefty as you might think. The coaching model below is simple and non-invasive, but it produces highly effective results in a very small amount of time—often ten minutes or less. It's an even simpler version of Footprint Leadership's one- to two-day, real-world, results-oriented coach training program for the time-strapped manager. And it can work for you even if employee development is simply not your forte. So if coaching just doesn't pique your interest, that's no problem. You don't have to be a brilliant coach. You might have gotten the impression from watching the work of external coaches coming into your organization that if you take up the coaching baton, you'll have to give up hours of your valuable work time or spend years studying the subtleties of the profession to have an impact. False. Internal coaching is actually entirely different from external coaching. You've got to manage the boss/employee dynamic we discussed earlier; the topics are different; the context is different; and you simply don't have the time an external coach has. It's about striking a balance between the SL as manager and the SL as coach, and that means that coaching time can be brief and to the point but still achieve tremendous results.

You might be familiar with Pareto's Law: 80 percent of the value comes from 20 percent of the input. This law could not be truer than in the coaching sphere. Indeed, some very simple coaching processes can yield you a lot of the value coaching has to offer without the years of training. A simple coaching process like the one I'll outline below can take the pressure off. You don't have to have all the answers; just trust the process, and you'll harvest a significant chunk of the value that coaching has to offer.

I'll share with you a fantastic example of what I mean by this. A colleague of mine named Larry took a computer language class years ago at Carnegie Mellon University. When it came time to take his final exam, Larry was in a state. He was convinced that he'd totally blown it and didn't have a hope in the world. The course outline was simple: "There are ten programming projects over the course of the semester. Two will be on the final exam. Complete the projects during the term, and you'll be ready for the final exam." Larry was bright, and he knew it—so he didn't attend any of the classes. But throughout the term, despite his efforts and his smarts, Larry couldn't get any of his programs to "compile." In other words, none of them worked. So, there he was at his final exam, sweating, and waiting to see which of the ten projects he knew he couldn't do would be on the test.

Before the students were allowed to begin, the professor shared these words of wisdom: "First, build your program to get a C grade on the exam. Then, once you've done that, add the features you think you need to get a B. And, if you have time, still more features for an A." Larry sat there stunned. He realized he'd spent the whole semester trying to build the ultimate program, gunning for the A right from the beginning. He consistently got bogged down in all the sophistication; he was trying to build the whole program at once, rather than starting with the foundation, working out the bugs, and then adding on to it. The pressure to perform was suddenly lifted; the exam was suddenly simple. What was Larry's final mark? An A, naturally.

Trying to produce the ultimate result or shooting for excellence can be daunting, complicated, slow, and in the worst case, paralyzing. It can also be downright inefficient. At point zero, before you begin, there are only so many variables that you can predict, manage, and plan for. Effective leadership is partly about acting in the face of ambiguity versus trying to control it by preparing for every possible outcome. As Albert Einstein said, "Any intelligent fool can make things bigger, more complex. It takes a touch of genius and a lot of courage to move it in the opposite direction." So, start simple, get started, and build from there.

I'm here to release you from the pressure to be a great coach. In the 1950s, the paediatrician and psychiatrist Donald Winnicott revolutionized the way that Americans approach parenting with his model of "The Good-Enough Mother." His idea was that you don't need to be perfect or superhuman to do a great job, and in fact, striving to be perfect often does more harm than good. His model is about allowing parents to be human, because being good enough is all their kids need from them. The same holds true for coaching. My model is not about spending huge amounts of time and always being able to ask the perfect question or provide the perfect nugget of wisdom to your EL. Instead, it's about just getting started and taking an honest crack at it. Or, as Larry learned, it's about starting with the basic model, and only expanding on that if you find you have the time and the inclination. For now, all I invite you to be is a Good-Enough Coach.

Before we go through the steps of my coaching model, I want

to make you aware of a filter that most SLs unconsciously bring into the coaching process. We discussed filters in the *Principle of Perspective* in chapter 12; they're perspectives through which we look at the world, often without noticing how much they change the picture, as with a pair of sunglasses you've worn for hours on a sunny day. The fact is that you, as a Senior Leader, will enter the coaching relationship with more experience, and presumably more knowledge from that experience, than the Emerging Leader you're coaching. This often leads to an SL, without necessarily being aware of it, adopting the filter, "I know better than the EL." If you're approaching the project from this perspective, it will seem natural for you to share your wisdom so they don't make the same mistakes you did—after all, it seems at the outset to be the most efficient way to get the task completed. But there are two serious drawbacks to this approach, which I call "dependency management," or the EL's consistently needing the SL's input in order to produce extraordinary results.

The first drawback is that often, an SL's greater level of experience actually creates a blind spot. It leads the SL into disregarding the EL's fresh perspective, although it might be perfectly valid and even superior, because the SL is unknowingly set in her ways and has become reliant on an approach that works for her. It has become a natural default in organizations for people to run with the first idea that comes to mind that isn't terrible and might work; often, these default ideas are only based on what's worked in the past. "If it's not broken, why fix it?"

I had to confront this same kind of blind spot in myself not too long ago, with a little input from my then two-and-a-half year old son, Simon. At that point, I had been driving for, say, twenty years. I know how to drive a car. You can criticize me for a lot of things, but I know how to drive. My son was in his car seat and I was driving him to nursery school. My wife usually takes him, but for some reason, she was unavailable that day. I had been to the school once before and I knew exactly where it was. Over the course of the school year, Simon had, of course, been there countless times.

As you can imagine, the road in front of the school at drop-off time was a complete zoo with the bustle of cars, buses, and kids everywhere, so I drove with extra caution. God forbid you hit a child. As you approach the school, there's a little turn to make into the parking lot. Right before that turn, there is a mini intersection. I was looking out for the turn into the parking lot and trying to see if there was an available parking space. I was not paying attention to the little intersection, and as the parking lot entrance was just beyond it, I didn't even see it. In the back, my two and a half year old son was saying "Stop, Daddy, stop!"

I wasn't listening.

"Stop, Daddy, stop!" he repeated, and in that second, I blew through the intersection, right through a stop sign. And I thought to myself, "I can't believe I did that!" It was a T-intersection, so I was fortunate that no car was approaching from the cross street.

I have been driving a car for twenty years, and this little wet-behind-the-ears kid in the back, was telling me to stop. He's never driven a car! But in reality, he had much more experience going to his school than I did. He knew that his mother always stopped at that particular location, just before reaching that intersection, on the way into the parking lot. I completely discounted his experience. In my mind, when he was telling me what to do, I was thinking, "Whatever, whatever. I'm the boss. I'm the driver here, okay?"

Indeed, it was all the experience I already had driving that completely blinded me to his fresh perspective, to the fresh eyes that he brought to this situation. I was so convinced by the filter that was unconsciously there ("I know how to drive, and Simon doesn't") that I was blinded to another reality: "Simon takes this route to school every day with his mother—even at two-and-a-half years old, he knows it better than I do."

This is a common pitfall for Senior Leaders: discounting the perspective of the EL. Incidentally, this "experience filter" also can be a common pitfall of ELs, in which they discount their own contribution to creating a solution because of their *lack* of experience. The combination of SLs offering their experience and ELs discounting theirs can set up a dynamic that leads us to the second drawback of dependency management.

The second drawback is that dependency keeps the EL from learning and growing, which will ultimately require greater amounts of your time and energy. As I mentioned before, if you keep handing them the fish, they've got no reason to learn to catch the fish themselves! I'll give you another example from the annals of parenting, but note that I use the parent/child relationship only as a metaphor. Obviously, the SL isn't a parent, and the EL isn't a child—yet a similar dynamic can emerge. What's closer to the truth is that involved parents who want to see their children gain independence often take on coaching roles, and so there's a certain level of transference for our purposes here.

There's a fantastic parenting philosophy created by Dr. Charles Fay and Jim Fay. It's based on the premise that you can't legislate good behaviour; rather, all people—adults and children alike—will only learn by consequences. As parents, it's natural for us to want to protect our children and help them do the best they can. But in doing that, we can actually take away their experience of learning. Instead, when it's appropriate and safe, we should allow them to take responsibility for their own choices by allowing them to experience the consequences of their actions, which will in turn shape their future behaviour.

For example, a lot of parents are veterans of the Coat War. It's wintertime; it's snowing outside, but little Madison doesn't want to put her coat on. Her father has to stuff her into the coat while she wiggles around and stamps her feet and makes an enormous scene. This episode repeats itself at the back door every day because, ultimately, the father "wins" every time, and Madison runs outside bundled up and unable to experience the consequence of *not* putting her coat on. Her father is only trying to say, "I care about you, and I don't want you to freeze," but he ends up dominating Madison's choices and limiting her understanding of the circumstances. We've all witnessed this situation deteriorate into a teeth-gritted shouting match when Madison chooses to make her stand not at the back door, but at the mall in full public view, where parents feel pressure to demonstrate some form of parental competence.

The simple solution is for her father to ask, "Okay, Madison, would you like to wear the coat or carry the coat?" Then the coat—and the consequences of wearing it or not wearing it—becomes Madison's problem, and Madison gets the satisfaction of choosing. If she chooses to carry it, she'll get outside, discover what it feels like to be cold in the snow, put the coat on, and the Coat War stalemate will be broken once and for all.

SLs often find themselves in the same pattern. They want to protect their ELs, their department, or—frankly—their own reputation as good managers (like the parent in the mall) from the consequences of the EL's mistakes. But in so doing, they limit the EL's opportunities for learning. There is no better time for ELs to make mistakes than now! First and foremost, your EL has gotten as far as he has because he's bright and capable and you recognized that, so the odds of his blowing a project completely are relatively small. But if you hover over him and give him all the right answers, soon enough, he'll get promoted from managing a project with a $100,000 budget to managing three people who have ten $100,000 projects each. Now he's managing multimillion-dollar portfolios, and you're no longer his direct superior. How can you guarantee that he's prepared for that level of responsibility unless you've allowed him to learn—and sometimes fail—when the stakes were comparably low?

This methodology doesn't mean that the SL is barred from providing input. You still have valuable experience and a broader context, and it's your job as a boss and mentor to pass this on. But before you do, I invite you to consider swapping your "I know better than the EL" filter for one that says, "*The EL is capable, and he or she is responsible for his or her own results*" (much like Madison and her coat). One filter is no more valid than the other, yet adopting the second will dramatically increase the latitude you give your EL, reduce the amount of experience-robbing advice you'd naturally want to give otherwise, and reduce the amount of time the EL needs from you, almost immediately.

There are, of course, times when you'll simply need to step in and offer your hard-earned knowledge. To return to the parenting analogy, when little Madison is about to run into a busy street, it's not a time to ask, "Madison, would you like to wait for the light to change, or try your luck?" It's a time to be direct, because the parent has judgment that Madison, in her limited experience, couldn't possibly have. I'll be the first to admit this is a difficult dance—learning when to step in and when not to. It is much like the job of a parent, who has to constantly let go a little more as their child's competency evolves and emerges. But you can learn to use your experience to discern between situations where the EL needs your direction and situations where you can allow the EL freedom to fail. If every project feels like a busy street to you, and you're the one making all the decisions, then you've got to ask yourself: Why did I hire the EL in the first place? Is the problem with the EL, the situation, or with me?

When you find yourself in a situation where the EL needs your input, the best idea is to stimulate her thinking rather than providing your answer. From your experience, you might know of a pitfall that an EL isn't aware of. You can start a conversation about it. "It looks like you're off to a great start. But have you considered what might happen if . . ." You do have greater knowledge, so you can poke and prod the EL's thinking into noticing situations that she doesn't have the experience to prepare for automatically. By asking questions and holding back your input (at least initially), however, you can send a message that says, "You can figure this out." That attitude not only instills confidence in the EL, but empowers them to rely on you less in the long run. They know you're not going to be serving up answers for them.

You also avoid throwing a wet blanket over their creativity by jumping in and saying, "No, no, you can't do it that way" or "This is the way it's always been done." The growing capability of the EL invariably leads to bolder thinking, actions, and results, and in turn increased confidence, which feeds the whole positive cycle. It might take some practice before you're comfortable enough with these risks so that your inner advice-giver agrees to take a vacation. To that end, I'd like to share the Navy's training line with Senior Leaders. How do you teach the new captains to turn a battle ship in the harbour? You tell them how to do it, and then you bite your tongue 'til it bleeds!

So we've seen how operating under the premise "the EL is capable and responsible for his or her own results" can be both a huge timesaver for you and a leadership development incubator for them. It'll also give you a big leg up in taking advantage of the simple coaching model below and becoming a "Good-Enough Coach."

The Good-Enough Coach

At the essence of this model are four coaching moments characterized by four questions: What's so? What's possible? What's missing? What's next? As we'll demonstrate, not all of the questions need to be asked. Indeed, asking is often just a part of the process that's needed to get the EL unstuck and moving forward. Let's look at each of the questions individually.

What's so?

"What's so?" is all about getting grounded in what's important and what the real issue is. "What happened?" or "What's the situation?" are similar questions. In North American business, there is a virtual epidemic of managers working feverishly to produce mediocre results on the wrong problems. Heike Bruch and Sumantra Ghoshal studied the behaviour of busy managers for ten years and published their ground-breaking findings in an article entitled "Beware the Busy Manager" in the *Harvard Business Review* in 2002. Their research revealed startling results: "Fully 90 percent of managers squander their time in all sorts of ineffective activities. In other words, a mere 10 percent of managers spend their time in a committed, purposeful, and reflective manner."

If your EL isn't clear on the challenge he is facing, time spent getting it clarified will be invaluable. The conversation is designed to begin with the "What's so?" question because, as much as possible, we want to get to the facts of the challenge your EL is facing. As we discussed in the last chapter, in the section on the *Principle of Perspective*, our interpretations of our experiences often become The Truth to us. You'll need to be very discerning about the difference between the EL's *opinion* about his experience and the actual *facts* of that experience—in essence, taking him out of the storytelling mode.

Say you ask, "What's so?" and the EL answers, "Joe will never buy into our approach."

"Did he use those words?" you respond.

"Well, not exactly," the EL says.

"What did Joe say specifically?"

"Actually, he said that the ROI of the new initiative wasn't clear and he didn't see how this was going to be a viable option."

"So he didn't actually say he'd never buy in, did he?" you ask.

"No, you're right," the EL says.

While the EL's interpretation in this example is a natural one, too often, we tend to buy into our interpretations and consider them absolute facts. That's a recipe for trouble, wouldn't you agree? If the EL's response is that Joe didn't see a clear ROI, he can now take the whole matter out of the subjective realm of storytelling—"he will never buy in"—and instead focus on the reality of the situation, such as how he could have performed better in the meeting or painted the ROI picture differently. "Maybe I didn't put my point of view across the way I could have," he might now think. "I could have done this, or I could have done that." Now the EL starts to think in a more grounded way about what the real issue is, instead of fixating on his interpretation of the situation.

Sometimes, of course, the issue doesn't present itself as clearly and comes out in a sea of issues. "Well, the presentation bombed, and Joe will never buy in. Bob just didn't seem to cooperate in the meeting and support where we're going as a group. I also think Dale could have done a better job preparing the presentation for us. I was also disappointed that our group just doesn't get the time it's promised on the agenda, and frankly, with the Anderson caseload, I didn't spend enough time getting ready myself. . . ." Many managers will inadvertently take this bait, jump in, and begin trying to solve the issue, either by systematically helping the EL move from one issue to the other or by going to work on the issue they have a ready answer for. It's tempting to dive in and rescue the EL. It's also far too much work, and you don't have the time. If you're honest, you're likely not yet aware of what the real issue is for the EL, either. Be lazy. After they load you with all the issues, ask *them* what they want to focus on. "What's the most important thing here? What will make the most difference? Where should we start? What's the real issue here?"

Once the EL is clear on what's so, and knows what the issue is, his or her thinking will naturally shift to what they want instead. Pause here, however, in the coaching. With the greater clarity about the issue, the most appropriate next steps often become evident to the EL. Don't work too hard; again, resist the temptation to jump in and "rescue" them from the situation. Remember, just be a Good-Enough Coach. Ask them, "Do you need anything else from me? Would working on this further with me be helpful?"

What's possible?

Whether the EL was already clear about the challenge when he came to you or you've just coached him to clarity, sometimes he'll get stuck on where to go from there. Perhaps he has no idea about what to do next, or perhaps his thinking is limited by a mediocre idea he already has. In either case, the options aren't particularly compelling until new possibilities are created.

You'll notice I keep banging my "don't rescue them" drum. That especially comes into play in this coaching moment, because the boss/employee dynamic can quickly dampen the creation of new ideas. After all, as the boss, your ideas can easily be interpreted by the EL as a directive about the way it should be done. As an SL, you want to continue to create the environment where the EL's ideas and input are welcome and appreciated by not prematurely leaping in with your own approach.

"What's possible?" is designed to shift the EL's thoughts from a problem focus into a solution focus and expand the number of options they already have. Like the other coaching moments, this one can be done in isolation. When done effectively, new potential solutions are generated very quickly and the most appropriate course of action is chosen.

Fresh thinking on creating fresh thinking. I want to present a fresh take on an old practice: creating new ideas. In corporate settings, we commonly refer to this as "brainstorming," and the experience is often a painful one comprised of pulling existing ideas out of peoples' heads and getting bogged down in debating each idea's merit. It's often a slow, meandering, and frustrating experience that results in a hodge-podge list of ideas circulated after the meeting, that don't go anywhere. It doesn't have to be that way—particularly not in coaching your EL. Brainstorming can be fresh, fruitful, and fast. In fact, it's remarkable what you can accomplish in ten minutes or less.

Why the brainstorming you're used to doesn't work—and what to do about it.

Pitfall #1: Getting trapped by existing ideas. Most idea-generating exercises start out on the right foot but end up on the wrong one—the same one, discussing existing ideas. In order to create new ideas, we need to first get the existing ones out on the table. This is where typical brainstorming starts off right. "Okay, so what ideas do you already have about how to approach this?" you might ask. Your EL or team puts in the ideas they already have. From there, the discussion typically goes one of two ways: you get bogged down in debating the merits of the ideas (see *Pitfall #2*), or one of the proposed existing and somewhat "it doesn't stink too badly so let's just go with it" ideas gets selected. In both scenarios, the idea creation stops before it really got going.

Solution. Table existing ideas. In order to create new ideas, we first empty our heads of the ideas we *already* have. Only then can we truly begin creating fresh thinking. Without debate or discussion, ask, “What ideas do you already have about this? . . . Anything else? . . . Anything?” You want to get to the bottom of the existing idea bin. Only when you hear, “Sorry, I’m out of ideas” are you ready to tap fresh ideas. But beware the second pitfall.

Pitfall #2: Getting bogged down. In creating new ideas, fast is good, very good. Here’s why: many of us are familiar with the fact that we have two sides of our brains—the left and the right. The left side is the logical, practical animal. It likes to analyze, gather data, and pull things apart to see how they work. It’s linear in how it processes and fabulous at being critical. The right side is the creative animal. Consider it like the “party” side of your brain. It loves a good time, it has few limits, is spontaneous, imaginative, and of course, creative. Instead of processing linearly, it’s a web processor; it’s brilliant at “connecting the dots,” seeing new things, and creating relationships between data, concepts, goals and the like.

The problem is that the left and right sides of the brain don’t get along too well, and using them at the same time bogs everything down. Just as the creative side gets revved up, creates a new idea and begins building on it, the logical side naturally wants to pick apart the idea, understand how it will work, and judge whether it’s any good—a complete creativity killer. The result? A small number of mostly existing ideas are batted about and torn apart with little new insight and no momentum.

Picture a bus moving along full of all the creative right brains. It’s a virtual party of new ideas; the conversation is flying. Then, somehow, one “practical” question slips in, and it slows the bus (the conversation) down. As soon as the bus slows down, the slower-moving, logical, practical left brains can start hopping on the bus and asking “practical” questions, slowing it down even more.

Before you know it, all the other logical buddies are on board, offering their analyses, and the creative conversation grinds to a halt. The trick to creating new possibilities is to keep the bus (and the conversation) moving quickly, very quickly. By doing this, our critical friends are never able to board the bus . . . until we invite them. In other words, engage the creative side of the brain first, then invite the logical side in to analyze and evaluate. The simplest and most effective way to do this? Speed.

Solution. Play the idea game. Only once all the existing ideas have been tabled, again, without discussion (say, two minutes in one-to-one coaching, slightly more in a group), and you've reached the bottom of the existing idea bin, play the idea game. Share the rules and objectives first.

Rules: The idea game is a no-holds-barred barrage of mental outflow: no morality, no practicality, no correct, no incorrect, no criticism, anything goes.

The core objective: To generate as many ideas as possible—it's about quantity, not quality. You declare a game of a certain number of ideas in a certain amount of time. My favourite starting point with one-to-one coaching conversations is six ideas in two minutes, but don't feel limited by that. You want to make it seemingly impossible to accomplish—it's astonishing how many ideas get created when seemingly there were no more to be had.

Pitfall #3: Not choosing the path forward. Now you've got a slew of ideas, or at least, far more than you had before. Likely there are a number of good new ones, or at minimum, confirmation that a previous idea was a strong one.

Solution. Effective action requires focus and selection; which idea to run with depends on what's most important at the time. With the ideas in mind, ask the questions that best fit your situation:

What's the cheapest?
What's the fastest?
What's the easiest?
What would have the most impact?
What's the most daring?

All of these are designed to spur the EL's thinking about the criteria of selecting the path for moving ahead. They culminate in the final question, "What *will* you do?" Big ideas are great. Challenging commitments can stretch, but if the EL isn't really prepared to act on them, they're not worth the exercise. We want to be clear on what the ELs will truly commit to.

What's missing?

As with the other coaching moments, this one can be done in isolation. The EL may be clear about the challenge and might have created a strong, overall idea on solving it, but he might still get bogged down in how to make it happen. He knows he's at Point A, and he knows he wants to get to Point B—so what's missing from his path? What does he need to get there? It's critical, however, that this conversation remain focused on the objectives and what the EL can do to change the situation. The Principle of Accountability applies here, as always. If the EL's answer to "What's missing?" is to say, "Well, Joe isn't cooperating," then without The Principle of Accountability, you've hit a wall. The problem (and power) is "over there" in some outside circumstance that needs to change. Rather than talking about what they believe *should* be, the focus needs to be brought back to what the EL can do and what's needed to impact change.

At any given time, we're all playing two games: an outer game and an inner game, just as a football player is simultaneously weaving through the linemen on the field and plotting his next move in his head. Your conversation about the EL's outer game will involve questions about the environment around you. Is the structure of the organization aligned to provide you with the support you need? Do you need more resources? Do you need help? Do we need to set a deadline? Do you need more commitment or buy-in? Often, what's missing in the outer game involves bridging gaps between people. Is there a conversation that's needed, and how would you like it to go?

The conversation about the EL's inner game is just as critical, but it's often overlooked because most SLs have so much experience with the outer game that this becomes their default. As you improve as a coach, you'll become just as adept at the inner game as you are at the outer game. The question to ask at this stage is, "What concerns do you have about this project?" A fear named is a fear tamed. The concerns are guaranteed to exist; they will always be there, but if the EL can first name them, then the next step to addressing them can be taken as opposed to pretending they don't exist and getting stopped by them anyway.

In this conversation, the *Principle of Immediacy* might come into play: how your EL behaves with you in discussing the project probably reflects how he is about the project in general. Does he appear excited, nervous, cautious, open, frustrated? Particularly if you sense something's off with your EL, use the technique of reflecting your immediate experience of the EL back to the EL. "I'm having the experience of X (ex. frustration/anxiety/annoyance/anger), as I'm sitting here with you. It seems like you are X. Is that accurate?" Checking in like this will allow you to take the conversation to the next level: So, what's missing now? How would you like to be about the situation as opposed to X?

The Immediacy conversation and the Accountability

conversation are the two most pivotal conversations you can have with your ELs as a manager and as a coach. Unfortunately, they're also the conversations most managers tend to avoid. They're afraid it might be uncomfortable or inappropriate. But in actuality, your ELs are craving an honest conversation and the opportunity to voice their concerns in a safe environment. Providing that environment for them will open the door to an entirely new world of results.

What's next?

Confucius said, "Man with open mouth wait long time for roast duck to fly in." Often, we sit around waiting for the perfect moment, the perfect boss, the perfect project, the perfect timing, or the perfect information that will allow us to commit, get us into action, and show the world how brilliant we are. Asking "What's next?" forces us to break this pattern of waiting for the perfect scenario, which will never arrive. You've identified with your EL what's needed externally and internally. Now all that's left is to identify the action to take, and then take it!

This section is the bridge between ideas created and the action taken. There are two key things that move any project forward quickly: promises and requests. If your EL promises, "I will get you the report by next Monday," or if your EL makes the request of someone else—"Will you get me the report by next Monday?"—the world shifts in that area, and we align our calendars, commitments, lives, etc. to fulfill that commitment. You start living toward a foreseeable future. Have you ever left a meeting where all kinds of great ideas were floated, but no promises or requests were made? In that situation where there's no next action defined, no matter how exciting the project, it gets trapped in limbo and it eventually dies. As an SL, you want to consistently make your own requests or solicit promises from the EL. Ask, "What's next? What's going to move the project forward? What does success look like? By when will it be done?" By doing this, you set up clear expectations and crisp accountability for both of you on which you can base your next coaching conversation. And then, when that promise or request is fulfilled, ask "What's next?" again and again.

It's really that simple. The easy "What's so? What's possible? What's missing? What's next?" process will make you a Good-Enough Coach in no time. By starting simple, as Larry did when trying to get his computer program to "compile," you can capture the bulk of value coaching has to offer, quickly and easily. Then, if you have the time or the interest, you can extend the conversation and go more deeply into your EL's fears and ambitions about this particular project or their career in general. But if a deeper conversation just isn't in the cards right now, no problem! You're already leaps and bounds ahead of the vast majority of Senior Leaders, and you'll see it proven time and again in your EL's confidence, morale, and performance. Starting the coaching conversation will transform your relationship with the Emerging Leaders in your organization, and you'll quickly see how this benefits their work, and your own as well.

14

The View from the Peak

We started chapter 1 from a precarious position. You were snow blind on Mt. Everest, struggling to get a crampon-hold and separated from your team of Emerging Leaders by an ever-widening crevasse. As much as you wanted to help your ELs rise behind you, you were climbing in the half-dark, without knowledgeable Sherpas to point out the way and help you run ladders across those communication gaps. To make matters worse, it wasn't always clear to you whether your ELs *wanted* to follow in your footsteps—half the time, they seemed to be waiting for the best moment to move on to Mt. Kilimanjaro, or to ditch mountaineering altogether!

It's my hope for you that this book has helped you find a path up the mountain. The apparent impasses between Senior Leaders and Emerging Leaders are largely a question of forging communication and understanding across the generation divide, and the fact that you picked up this book in the first place was a major step in the right direction. Now that you've made it to the last chapter—reached the peak of Mt. Everest, as it were—you can look back on that slippery and fraught climb with clarity, and look forward into the bright vista of the future. In the past, you might have felt bewildered by or even disappointed in your Emerging Leaders, who didn't seem to approach your organization with focus or seriousness. During the work week, they could be scatterbrained and distracted, or, even more baffling, they were so direct and disregarding of office politics that they struck you as arrogant and entitled. To top off this seemingly brazen attitude, you were lucky to get a glimpse of their backs scooting out the door before six p.m., and if you ran into an emergency over the weekend, the best you could hope for was to reach their breezy voicemail recording saying, "I'm heading to the triathlon in Phoenix—my Blackberry will be turned off until Monday!" If you were anything like the many Senior Leaders I've worked with, getting a foothold in this environment seemed frustrating at best and impossible at worst.

But now, here we are at the peak. You now understand Emerging Leaders as young men and women confronting a shifting society that leaves them overextended between work, children, personal relationships, and personal ambitions outside your organization—things that might never have factored into your priorities, like flying to Phoenix for a triathlon. Changing gender dynamics mean that both your male and female ELs can't rely on a stay-at-home spouse to run the household, and so they're facing to-do lists that include not only the work priorities you've outlined for them, but also vacuuming, preparing for the neighbourhood potluck, and attending little Rebecca's ballet recital. And for the first time in generations, these concerns might take precedence over workplace manoeuvring. Your ELs watched their parents—usually their fathers—pay a high personal price for their heavy professional focus, and they're not keen on following suit.

Not only are you now able to see more clearly what the EL's life looks like outside the nine-to-five bracket and why they might be so eager to get out of the office, but you've also got a better understanding of what motivates them when you do have their attention. The work ethic of nose-to-the-grindstone sacrifice that got many SLs where they are today simply doesn't light a fire under your ELs. You work for the company, but they work for Me, Inc. They're loyal to their personal lives first and their careers second, and their careers will take precedence over the company. Climbing the professional ladder no longer means sticking it out with one organization, paying dues for small returns in incremental promotions. ELs need to ensure that Me, Inc. remains marketable, and they will change organizations to get those needs met. And if they do stand still with one company for any length of time, it's likely because they've formed a loyalty to their boss, not to the organization as a whole. The job security of yesterday isn't enough of a dangling carrot for ELs anymore. Indeed, today there are no companies that can truly offer job security anyway. Businesses are facing more and more change at an ever-increasing rate. When people see the likes of General Motors and Merrill Lynch face bankruptcy, require bailouts, or both, the need to think about Me, Inc. is simply the smart thing to do.

In today's talent economy and world of change, opportunities abound for Emerging Leaders. Unlike many SLs, who have lived to work, ELs work to live and enjoy the fruits outside of their professional lives such as family, fitness, learning, personal growth, and service to the community.

All of these changes represent a marked shift in the business culture, and may strike some Senior Leaders as foreign. But the good news is that simply getting a picture of your ELs' differing worldview and attitudes gets you halfway across the communication divide. And over the course of this book, we've done even better than that—not only are you now better equipped to understand your ELs' perspectives, you also have the tools with which to approach them, have meaningful exchanges with them, and get them on board to do the best they can for you and your organization.

Now that you understand the ELs' daily trials and triumphs, you know how to cut them a break when they need it and offer what most matters to them. This isn't to say that getting to the top of Mt. Everest means turning your office on its head, so that it's all about the ELs and their needs. Instead, you've learned to speak the ELs' language, so that you can offer them what they need and want most in exchange for their best work. Everyone comes out on top, together.

The view from the peak of Mt. Everest is of an organization where Senior Leaders and Emerging Leaders produce extraordinary results together in the context of partnership. Everyone takes accountability, acknowledging their own successes and failures. Communication is of the utmost importance, so that you as a Senior Leader are constantly abreast of what matters to your Emerging Leaders, and they, in turn, are willing to update you with their progress and make requests when help is necessary. Your ELs manage themselves and take responsibility for their results; they don't need constant surveillance, but they willingly come to you to benefit from your experience and guidance. It's a beautiful view, and the future is bright for your business.

It's my hope that the guidance in this book has paved the way for better functioning relationships with the Emerging Leaders of your organization, a deeper bench of committed and talented leaders, and greater confidence that these emerging leaders will begin to add unprecedented value to your organization—not someday, but now.

Best of luck to you—and enjoy the view from the peak!

Ideas are Meant to be Shared

Seth Godin is a leading thinker about marketing and leadership, but what he really does is challenge the status quo for a living. He also inspires me tremendously. I began this book with a quote from him, so it's appropriate that I end with one from him as well.

What follows is part of what he wrote on his blog in May 2008 about making the most out of business books:

"It's not about you. It's about the next person. The single best use of a business book is to help someone else. Sharing what you read, handing the book to a person who needs it . . . pushing those around you to get in sync and to take action—that's the main reason it's a book, not a video or a seminar. A book is a souvenir and a container and a motivator and an easily leveraged tool. Hoarding books makes them worth less, not more.

"Effective managers hand books to their team. Not so they can be reminded of high school, but so that next week she can say to them, 'Are we there yet?'"

If you found *The Emerging Leader* useful, don't store it away somewhere and let it collect dust. Pass it along to someone you think might benefit.

Are Your Emerging Leaders Ready to Become the Future of Your Business?

You can create outstanding commitment and performance from your future leaders faster and easier than you think. It's time to learn how to form a deeper and more loyal bench of talent than you currently have.

Footprint Leadership specializes in unlocking the talent, potential and value of your firm's Emerging Leaders. We offer a variety of services designed to help organizations grow, leverage and retain their future leaders quickly and effectively. Our clients are forward-thinking firms that have engaged in succession planning and are committed to developing the leadership capacity of their organizations.

Footprint Leadership services include:

- ☐ **EXECUTIVE COACHING**—Tailored, 1:1, ROI oriented coaching designed to accelerate your select emerging leaders' capabilities fast.
- ☐ **GROUP LEADERSHIP PROGRAMS**—In-house, transformational experiences for groups of Emerging Leaders that cause leadership, not just talk about it.
- ☐ **CREATE YOUR OWN COACHES**—Have your managers coach effectively in 10 minutes or less with real-world, in-house coaching solutions for the time-strapped manager.
- ☐ **KEYNOTES, WORKSHOPS AND WEBINARS**—Spice up your conferences, retreats and in-house events with dynamic and practical presentations on leadership topics.
- ☐ **CONSULTING**—Tap the value of your future leaders with advice from experienced, in-the-trenches Emerging Leader specialists.

"I look at Footprint as an accelerant to developing our leaders. You help them reach their potential far faster and that's of great value to us . . . I have no doubt that there will be success at the end of each engagement."

—Sherry Duffy, Senior HR Executive

See the following page for the Footprint Leadership Special Bonuses offer.

FREE BONUSES! $485 VALUE

SPECIAL BONUSES

As a "thank you" for purchasing *The Emerging Leader* , you're entitled to get these FREE resources (valued at $485) now from author Jamie Broughton:

1. **THE LEADERSHIP SPRINGBOARD WORKBOOK**. Discover the essential building blocks of leadership that our programs and client successes are built on—a timeless resource for any Emerging Leader.

2. **THE BEST FIT INDEX**. Quickly gauge the likelihood that investing in your leadership development candidate(s) will generate the ROI your company deserves.

3. **SUBSCRIPTION** to Jamie's *Footnotes* publication. Get an authentic insider's perspective on what it really takes to lead: unconventional, short, and thought-provoking stories about leadership and high-performance.

4. **THE EMERGING LEADER STRATEGY SESSION**. Whether you're planning a full-scale program or simply considering coaching for yourself or select individual(s), you'll leave this phone session clear and excited about what's possible.

To collect your free resources simply visit
www.EmergingLeaderBook.com/bonus

Contact us at:
info@FootprintLeadership.com
1-866-968-6275
www.FootprintLeadership.com

To order additional copies of *The Emerging Leader*
or take advantage of our bulk discounts,
please visit **www.EmergingLeaderBook.com**